CU00925577

The selected poems of Joanna Baillie
1762–1851

MANCHESTER
UNIVERSITY PRESS

The selected poems of Joanna Baillie
1762–1851

Edited by Jennifer Breen

Manchester University Press

Manchester and New York

distributed exclusively in the USA by St. Martin's Press

Copyright © Jennifer Breen 1999

The right of Jennifer Breen to be identified as the editor of this work has been asserted by her in accordance with the Copyright Designs and Patents Act 1988.

Published by Manchester University Press
Oxford Road, Manchester M13 9NR, UK
and Room 400, 175 Fifth Avenue, New York, NY 10010, USA
http://www.man.ac.uk/mup

Distributed exclusively in the USA by
St. Martin's Press, Inc., 175 Fifth Avenue, New York,
NY10010, USA

Distributed exclusively in Canada by
UBC Press, University of British Columbia, 6344 Memorial Road,
Vancouver, BC, Canada V6T 1Z2

British Library Cataloguing-in-Publication Data
A catalogue record for this book is available from the British Library

Library of Congress Cataloging-in-Publication Data applied for

ISBN 0 7190 5474 5 *hardback*

First published 1999

06 05 04 03 02 01 00 99   10 9 8 7 6 5 4 3 2 1

Typeset by Bryan Williamson, Frome, Somerset
Printed in Great Britain
by Bookcraft (Bath) Ltd, Midsomer Norton

Contents

List of illustrations

Acknowledgements

I am grateful to Matthew Frost and Stephanie Sloan at Manchester University Press for all their editorial help. I also wish to thank R. W. Noble for his literary advice; and Marjorie Edwards for her word-processing of the Notes in this book. I am also grateful to Dr Iain G. Brown, National Library of Scotland; Deborah Hunter, Picture Library, National Galleries of Scotland; Lizzie MacGregor, Scottish Poetry Library; Dr Oliver S. Pickering, Brotherton Library at the Leeds University Library; and Katrina Thomson, National Gallery of Scotland; as well as to staff at the British Library and the Department of Manuscripts; Hamilton District Library; the London Library; the John Rylands University Library at the University of Manchester; the National Portrait Gallery; the Royal College of Surgeons of England Library; and the Learning Centre at the University of North London.

Introduction

Joanna Baillie's authorship and the canon of Romantic poetry

My *Selected Poems of Joanna Baillie* gives readers a modern edition of Baillie's poems with notes which explain historical and other allusions. I have included most of the poems in her first volume, *Poems* (1790),[1] which she published anonymously, and five of the six poems that she contributed to the anthology that she edited, *A Collection of Poems* (1823),[2] as well as a number of poems from her *Fugitive Verses* (1840),[3] which she compiled after discovering that some of her earlier poems were being pirated in various anthologies without acknowledgement of her authorship. In addition, I have included a few more poems that Baillie, towards the end of her life, collected in her *Dramatic and Poetical Works* (1851).[4] My concern in this book is with Baillie's lyric poetry, of which I have here selected fifty-two poems that are of literary merit and yet excluded from the received canon of Romantic poetry.

After Joanna Baillie oversaw the publication of her collected *Dramatic and Poetical Works* in 1851, a few of her poems were later anthologized by nineteenth-century and early twentieth-century editors.[5] But her poems during recent times have scarcely been referred to in literary histories or anthologies. The *New Cambridge Bibliography of English Literature*, for example, omits Joanna Baillie's poetry, but gives bibliographies of the poetry of several of her contemporaries such as Anna Barbauld, Anna Seward and Charlotte Smith.[6] Nevertheless, since Roger Lonsdale made his 1984 discovery of Baillie's anonymously published *Poems* (1790),[7] and since my publication of several of Baillie's major poems in my *Women Romantic Poets, 1785-1832: An Anthology* (1992, new edn 1994), a renewal of interest in Joanna Baillie's poems has begun. In 1994, when Jonathan Wordsworth reprinted a facsimile edition of Baillie's first book, *Poems* (1790), in his 'Revolution and Romanticism Series, 1789-1834', he commented, 'Baillie, like the Wordsworth of *Lyrical Ballads*, is funny, sad, tender, affectionate, capable of many moods, of "passion genuine and true to nature" . . . She had it in her to be a poet of real stature.'[8] In contrast with Jonathan Wordsworth, I argue that Joanna Baillie *is* a poet of real stature.

In support of this argument, my selection offers readers a full range of the best of Baillie's poems: meditative lyrics such as 'A Winter Day' and 'A Summer Day'; dramatic monologues such as 'A Disappointment' and

'A Reverie'; domestic and personal poems such as 'A Mother to Her Waking Infant' and 'To Mrs Siddons'; Scots English songs such as 'Hooly and Fairly', 'Tam o' the Lin', and 'The Gowan Glitters on the Sward'; and songs with a Welsh or Irish source of inspiration such as 'O Welcome Bat and Owlet Gray', 'The Black Cock', 'The Morning Air Plays on my Face' and 'His Boat Comes on the Sunny Tide'.

In this volume, I have not reprinted any of Baillie's plays in blank verse because these are a different genre and because it is important at this stage of Baillie studies to reclaim her lyric poetry, much of which predates her plays, but has been overshadowed by her dramas which were more popular in her own day and continue to be so with literary critics today. Also, I have not included any of Baillie's *Metrical Legends of Exalted Characters* (1821) and *Ahalya Baee* (1851) because these excursions into stereotypical varieties of 'orientalism' are long narratives in a different genre.[9]

Joanna Baillie's life and the critical reception of her work
Joanna Baillie (1762-1851) was born at Bothwell, Lanarkshire, Scotland, in her father's parish church manse overlooking the valley of the River Clyde. Her twin sister died at birth. Until she was seven, Joanna lived at Bothwell with her parents, Dorothea Hunter Baillie and James Baillie, and her older sister, Agnes, and her brother, Matthew. Then her father, a minister in the main Church of Scotland tradition, transferred with his family to a nearby church in Hamilton. At the age of ten, Joanna and her sister were sent to a boarding-school in Glasgow. Here Joanna learned the three Rs as well as geography and history. She also learned to sing and to accompany herself on the guitar, and, in fact was said to excel in vocal and instrumental music.[10]

In 1776, the Baillies moved to Glasgow on the appointment of James Baillie as a Professor of Divinity at the University of Glasgow, but he died suddenly two years later. In the following year, 1779, Joanna and her mother and sister moved to Mrs Baillie's childhood home, Long Calderwood, which Mrs Baillie's family, the Hunters, had owned for generations. At this small country estate outside Glasgow, Joanna observed and participated in the flourishing local Scots folk musical culture. In a letter of 1822 to George Thomson, she recalled 'Hooly and Fairly' as 'a tune I used formerly to sing along with the guitar'.[11]

In 1779, Matthew Baillie took up a fellowship in order to study medicine at Balliol College, Oxford, and a year later he entered the Hunter School of Anatomy, Windmill Street, London, which belonged to his uncle, William Hunter, who was renowned for his discoveries in obstetrics.

When Dr William Hunter died in 1783, Matthew Baillie inherited his London home in Windmill Street, along with the Windmill Street School of Anatomy as well as the family estate at Long Calderwood. Long Calderwood was subsequently conveyanced to Matthew's uncle, John Hunter, in order to resolve an old dispute between the Hunter brothers. Joanna with her mother and sister had to leave Long Calderwood and move south to live with Matthew in his Windmill Street house in London.[12] Matthew Baillie subsequently developed a lucrative medical practice which led to his appointment as a physician to King George III from 1810 until the king's death in 1820.

In 1783, Joanna Baillie was thus suddenly transferred from rural Scotland to London, where she established herself in a literary social circle, which was in part facilitated by attendance at the *conversazione* of Anne Hunter, her aunt by marriage. Although Baillie had been experimenting with Scots English song-writing at Long Calderwood, in her early London years she wrote her first complete book, *Poems: Wherein It Is Attempted to Describe Certain Views of Nature and Rustic Manners* (1790), which she published anonymously with the radical publisher, Joseph Johnson. This work sold only a few copies, despite the fact that it received a favourable review in the *Monthly Review* (November 1791). William Enfield, the reviewer, wrote, '[Baillie's lyric poems] . . . have little of that richness of melody which, in many of our modern poets, so sweetly captivates the ear: but they contain minute and circumstantial descriptions of natural objects, scenes, and characters; and they express, in easy though peculiar language, the feelings of undisguised and uncorrupted nature.'[13] Fifty years later, after anthologists had reprinted some of these early poems, Baillie reissued many of them in her collection of lyric poetry, *Fugitive Verses* (1840).

Baillie herself, in her 'Preface' to *Fugitive Verses* (see Appendix 2, p.195), commented on the dearth of major new poetry in the early 1790s, and on her failure to promote her own *Poems* (1790) which might have won her a reputation then as a lyric poet:

> When these [1790] poems were written, the author was young in years, and still younger in literary knowledge. Of all our eminent poets of modern times, not one was then known. Mr. Hayley and Miss Seward, and a few other cultivated poetical writers, were the poets spoken of in literary circles. Burns, read and appreciated as he deserved by his own countrymen, was known to few readers south of the Tweed, where I then resided . . . I have, perhaps, no great reason to regret that my vanity was not stirred up at that time to more active exertions.

If Baillie's 1790 poems had been distributed and sold more widely at the time of their first publication, early nineteenth-century readers might have recognized the evocativeness of her language and the authenticity of her representations of country labouring and farming people. These poems carried forward the enlightened notion of using a less artificial and more direct language in poetry and broadening the subject matter of elevated or literary poetry in order to include ordinary men and women in their every-day work and relationships.

As Marilyn Butler demonstrates convincingly, William Wordsworth was not the complete innovator that critics often claim him to be: 'We should dismiss at the outset the belief, still widely held, that Wordsworth's contributions to the *Lyrical Ballads* of 1798 represent an altogether new kind of poetry. Wordsworth's experiments with subjects among the lower orders of society, in metres appropriately taken from popular poetry, follow thirty years of public interest in this matter and this manner, and are thus characteristic of the culture of the Enlightenment.'[14] Butler mentions Thomas Percy's *Reliques of Ancient English Poetry* (1765) as a starting-point; and Baillie in her 1790 *Poems* can be seen as much a pioneer of 'experiments with subjects among the lower orders of society' as Words-worth. In fact, in relation to her writing of drama, Baillie demonstrated theoretically this point in the very year that Wordsworth's and Coleridge's *Lyrical Ballads* appeared. Baillie wrote: 'those strong passions that, with small assistance from outward circumstances, work their way in the heart, till they become the tyrannical masters of it, carry on a similar operation in the breast of the monarch, and the man of low degree.'[15]

Baillie seems to have decided against becoming a lyric poet when her first book failed to sell in 1790. Instead, she turned to the writing of drama in blank verse. She discovered that the reading public were interested in these dramas, though she found it difficult to get many of them staged. Today those dramas still attract more critical mention than her lyric poetry does. Stuart Curran, for example, when he surveyed women writers of the Romantic period, stated, 'her three-volume *Series of Plays; in which it is Attempted to Delineate the Stronger Passions of the Mind* (1798-1812), was hailed in comparison to Shakespeare and, of all contemporary influences, exerted the most direct practical and theoretical force on serious drama written in the Romantic period'.[16] Nowadays, opinions diverge widely about the value of Baillie's and other Romantic drama, but there is univer-sal agreement about the merit of Romantic lyric poetry, a genre in which Baillie can increasingly be seen as an important practitioner.

All the major poems in her 1790 volume show her interest in the rural life of her father's parishioners and the tenant farmers on her mother's family's estate. Her blank verse poems, 'A Winter Day' and 'A Summer Day' (1790), for example, celebrate the working lives of smallholding yeomanry in the Scottish lowlands. In an unpublished manuscript, *Recollections Written at the Request of Miss Berry* (1831), Baillie describes how she had the opportunity to observe 'labouring and country people':

> Traits in human nature whether in books or in real life have always had most power in arresting my attention and keeping place in my recollection. This has often made me a watcher of children at play or under any excitement, and/or frequenter in early life of the habitations of labouring and country people which happily for me I had many opportunities of doing. I might forget the dialogue in which it was displayed and could not therefore make a truthful anecdote of it, but the trait itself remained perhaps forever.[17]

Here Baillie shows how she got in touch with the actual lives of the people whom she describes in detail; for example she is at once humorous as well as sympathetic and accurate in her evocations, which range from the yeoman's dreams – which leave him 'just the same poor man / As when he went to rest' – to the children at play:

> One on the ice must try his new soled shoes:
> To view his well-set trap another hies,
> In hopes to find some poor unwary bird
> (No worthless prize) entangled in his snare;
> Whilst one, less active, with round rosy face,
> Spreads out his purple fingers to the fire,
> And peeps, most wishfully, into the pot.

These rural people – the farmer and his three children – are individualized so that their behaviour shows motivation and vivacity. Thus Baillie's first poems represent country people more realistically than the more generalized figures of the common people who are described in some of the earlier eighteenth-century verse, such as Oliver Goldsmith's *The Deserted Village* (1770):

> How often have I paused on every charm,
> The sheltered cot, the cultivated farm,
> The never-failing brook, the busy mill,
> The decent church that topped the neighbouring hill,
> The hawthorn bush, with seats beneath the shade,
> For talking age and whispering lovers made.[18]

The narrator of this elegiac poem expresses generalities about the village which serve to distance himself and his reader from his subject. In contrast, Baillie particularizes the singular characteristics of the family whom she is describing.

Baillie was of course no more the sole progenitor of a new Romantic poetry than Wordsworth was; if we compare the generalized verse of William Cowper in the 1780s with the more specific poetry of Stephen

Duck in 1730, we find that 'Romanticism' had its roots much earlier in the eighteenth century. Cowper, in his long blank verse poem, *The Task* (1785) celebrates rural pleasures, and unlike Goldsmith, demonstrates a sympathy for the working poor, whom he succeeds in characterizing to some extent:

> Forth goes the woodman, leaving unconcerned
> The cheerful haunts of man; to wield the axe
> And drive the wedge, in yonder forest drear,
> From morn to eve his solitary task.[19]

But already by 1730, the labourer-poet, Stephen Duck, had in *The Thresher's Labour* mocked the pastoral conventions of representing the countryside as inherently refreshing and specifies the grim reality of the thresher's work: 'When sooty pease we thresh, you scarce can know / Our native colour, as from work we go . . .'.[20]

George Crabbe also, particularly in *The Village* (1783), represents English labouring life in dismal colours. In the following excerpt, Crabbe attacks the fantasies of those writers and readers who subscribe to the notion of 'rural ease' and 'wholesome' plenty:

> Oh! trifle not with wants you cannot feel,
> Nor mock the misery of a stinted meal;
> Homely not wholesome, plain not plenteous, such
> As you who envy would disdain to touch.
>
> Ye gentle souls who dream of rural ease . . .
> Go look within, and ask if peace be there:
> If peace be his – that drooping weary sire
> Or theirs, that offspring round their feeble fire,
> Or hers, that matron pale, whose trembling hand
> Turns on the wretched hearth the expiring brand.[21]

Crabbe's use of adjectives here, however, seem part of his satiric attack on those more well-off poet-observers who have no genuine interest in the poor, rather than an engagement with discovering appropriate language for conveying the actual lives of his subjects.[22] In contrast, Baillie's children at play are described in plain language: the first tries sliding on the ice in his 'new-soled shoes'; the second investigates his 'well-set trap' to see whether he has caught a bird; and the third anticipates breakfast by looking 'most wishfully, into the pot'. These lines capture the imaginative lives of these children; and her emphasis on the 'pastoral' does not mitigate against the strength of her realistic detailing of country people's lives.

Baillie reflects the interests of many Scottish Renaissance thinkers and late eighteenth-century English dissenters who theorized about the nature of the world of childhood and about how the mind developed. For Baillie, her analyses of human emotion and feeling which she expressed in her 1790 *Poems*, became central to her later theories about art.[23] By 1798, Baillie had formulated her theoretical ideas about the necessity of portraying human feeling in poetry:

> The fair field of what may properly be called poetry, is enriched with so many beauties, that in it we are tempted to forget what we really are and what kind of beings we belong to . . . I will venture, however, to say, that amidst all this decoration and ornament, all this loftiness and refinement, let one simple trait of the human heart, one expression of passion genuine and true to nature, be introduced, and it will stand forth alone in the boldness of reality, whilst the false and unnatural around it, fades away upon every side, like the rising exhalations of the morning.[24]

Baillie here indicates her belief that poetry, if it is to move the reader, should be concerned with the 'genuine' feelings and behaviour of the common man and woman rather than with the 'artificial', cultivated feelings 'of the more refined part of society'. Baillie had already succeeded in putting her views into practice in her 1790 *Poems*, and she published her theories about poetry two years prior to Wordsworth's similarly worded *Preface* to the second edition of his and S. T. Coleridge's *Lyrical Ballads* (1800).

Baillie was therefore, with Stephen Duck and Robert Burns, among the first of eighteenth-century poets to empathize with her subjects – in her case, the smallholding farmers and village labourers whom she had observed as a child at Bothwell and Hamilton as well as during adolescence on her mother's family estate at Long Calderwood near Glasgow. In depicting members of the Scottish yeomanry and various villagers, whose way of life was under threat from the consolidation of agriculture in the hands of large landowners, she engaged with some of the conventions of eighteenth-century English pastoral poetry but she specified the actual details of rural life and she did so with a less elevated diction than that of poets such as Oliver Goldsmith, William Cowper and George Crabbe. Although by 1822 she had met Crabbe through the banker, Samuel Hoare, who lived near her in Hampstead, and Crabbe visited her to read her his latest poems,[25] she seems not to have been influenced by his work in the way that Sir Walter Scott's retelling of medieval legends in, for example, 'The Lay of the Last Minstrel' encouraged Baillie to write *Metrical Legends of Exalted Characters* (1821) and her Scottish historical drama, *The Family Legend*.[26] Baillie must have been aware of Crabbe's poem, *The Village* (1783), which in part satirizes neo-classical pastoral poetry, but in 1840, when she came to revise some of her 1790 *Poems*, she did not alter her realistically detailed pictures of pastoral equilibrium in 'A Winter Day', 'A Summer Day' and other poems.

Joanna Baillie's use of standard English and Scots English
Joanna Baillie's writing of poetry probably began with her composition of
Scottish songs and ballads in her late adolescence in 1779 at Long Calderwood, Lanarkshire. Margaret Carhart notes that 'during the years at Long
Calderwood, she [Baillie] had begun to write clever Scotch ballads and
adaptations of old songs, which were sung round the ingle hearths of the
neighbourhood'.[27] Baillie's composition of new or revised versions of old
ballads formed part of that eighteenth-century resurgence of interest by
the Scots in their own traditional language and literature. The interest in
the recovery or reworking of Scottish airs was particularly strong between
the time of Allen Ramsay's *Tea-Table Miscellany* (1724) up to the years
when Herd's *Ancient and Modern Scottish Songs* (1776, 1791) became
popular. It was at this time that James Johnson (*c*.1750-1811), principal
music engraver in Scotland at the end of the eighteenth century, invited
Robert Burns (1759-1796), Baillie's contemporary, to contribute songs to
his series, *The Scots Musical Museum*, which eventually ran to six volumes
(1787-1803). Burns agreed enthusiastically, because Johnson wished to
reprint the authentic 'favourites of Nature's Judges – the Common
People'.[28]

Burns was less enthusiastic in 1792 about collaborating with another
anthologist of Scottish songs, George Thomson (1757-1851), who worked
for the Board of Trustees for the Encouragement of Manufactures. Burns
agreed to contribute to Thomson's project, though he suspected that
Thomson would erode the authenticity of the songs. Thomson had confided
to Burns that he wanted to 'present the Public with a collection . . . accept-
able to all persons of taste . . .'[29] Only the first volume of Thomson's *A
Select Collection of Scottish Airs* (1793), however, had been published
before Burns died in 1796.

In his editorial 'Preface' to his *Collection of the Songs of Burns, Sir
Walter Scott, Bart, and other Eminent Lyric Poets* (1822), Thomson relates
how after Burns's death he had to look elsewhere for his contributors: 'On
the lamented death of Burns, the Editor, after a considerable pause, sought
and fortunately obtained the assistance of Joanna Baillie, Mrs Grant, Mrs
John Hunter, Sir Alexander Boswell, Sir Walter Scott, and William
Smyth'.[30] From 1804, Thomson commissioned from Baillie approximately
twenty original or adapted poems for Scottish, Irish and Welsh melodies;
he published these in various separate anthologies from 1809 to 1816,
which he combined into his six-volume collection of 1822.

When Thomson first approached Baillie about writing and adapting
lyrics for traditional Welsh, Irish and Scottish airs, she responded self-
deprecatingly,

to the friend of [Robert] Burns and my own countryman, it is impossible to refuse, in such a work as you are engaged in, any little assistance that I am able to give . . . I shall do it as well as I can; but as I have really neither the elegance nor the skill in musical numbers that are required for this kind of writing, and should never in my life have written a single song if I had not wanted one for my own particular purposes, you must not be surprised if those I send you should not prove exactly what you would wish.[31]

Baillie was already forty-two when she began to write songs of Irish and Welsh inspiration as well as Scots English songs for Thomson's collections of traditional songs. But she could nevertheless draw on her knowledge of the Scottish airs and folk culture of her early years in Lanarkshire. If Thomson had not commissioned these original and adapted poems for traditional melodies, Baillie might not have composed any poems of Welsh or Irish inspiration nor indeed many poems in Scots English, yet this entire group of poems comprise one of her enduring claims to our attention.

Because Baillie grew up in a highly educated household and attended school in Glasgow as well as mixing with her father's parishioners and, later, the farming community around Long Calderwood, she was conversant with both standard English and modern Scots English. But by 1804, she had settled in Hampstead village and moved mostly within its closed literary and professional circle, so that she had to rely on memory for creating Scots English usage. She was also aware of the possessive feelings that Scottish people had for their traditional songs, and she realized that radically different versions might at times alienate her audience.

In relation to the poems that Thomson asked her to write for the Irish and Welsh airs he chose, her main difficulties arose from her lack of knowledge of the languages and cultures of these very different nations. She therefore had to write those poems in standard English. Although she visited Wales in 1814, she mainly relied on research into books on travel, such as William Gilpin's *Observations on the River Wye* (1782), as well as on her musical friends and relations, rather than experiencing Irish and Welsh culture to any great extent herself.

Her initial attempts at poems for George Thomson were a response to his commission for poems to be set to Welsh airs for his *Collection of Welsh Airs*, 1. Baillie was not familiar with Welsh or Irish Celtic languages, so she composed these poems in standard English. Her letters to Thomson reveal the difficulties that she had in suiting her poetic skills to Thomson's wishes.

Thomson wished to use Baillie's poems, which she agreed to give him without contractual payment, but he tried to persuade Baillie to make what he considered to be necessary alterations in some of her phrasing. Thomson based his suggested emendations on aesthetic, linguistic, or musical grounds, but Baillie often demurred, insisting on her choice of language or metrical arrangement. In relation to 'O welcome bat and owlet gray', for instance, which was one of the first poems that Baillie sent him in 1804, she refused to alter her third line from 'O welcome moth and drowsy fly' to 'O welcome every drowsy fly':

> I am sorry not to alter the line to your taste as I am sure, from your writing expressly about this line, there must be something in the word *moth* really disagreeable to your ear. If this be so, I have no objection to your altering the line as you propose; but then you must have the goodness in a note at the bottom of the page where it is printed to mention that you have altered it, and to give the line there as I originally wrote it. In this way your readers, or rather your singers will choose for themselves; and, if your line should become more popular than mine, I shall not at all be offended.[32]

Thomson did not publicize their editorial dispute in this manner, however, and Baillie's line remained unaltered.

Thomson also tried to make Baillie eschew humour, particularly in relation to her Welsh and Irish poems. The second poem that Baillie sent Thomson in 1804, for example, which at first was known as 'The Maid of Lanwellyn', concluded with the following stanza:

> The neighbours lament that I'm clownish and shy,
> And my limbs are too long and nose is awry.
> I thank you, good neighbours, but so let me be,
> Since the Maid of Lanvilling smiles sweetly on me.[33]

Baillie complained that, although she had already altered her poem substantially, she found it difficult to meet Thomson's requirements:

> I come now to my own little matters regarding this same perverse *Maid of Lanvilling*, whom I cannot get properly tricked out as she should be, let me take ever so much pains upon her. It is not that *I canna be fashed*, but really and truly *I canna do ne mair*. As for the last stanza which you may think inferior to the rest, I must e'en in the sturdy spirit of an author say that I think it is rather the best of them all tho' I am willing enough to admit there is not one of them very good.

But Thomson eventually persuaded her to delete her humorous 'Lanvilling' and to transform her maid's suitor into a somewhat more decorous character.[34] Baillie's final version met with Thomson's approval:

> The farmer rides proudly to market or fair,
> The clerk at the alehouse still claims the great chair,
> But, of all our proud fellows, the proudest I'll be,
> While the Maid of Llanwellyn smiles sweetly on me?

> For blithe as the urchin at holyday play,
> And meek as a matron in mantle of gray,
> And trim as a lady of gentle degree,
> Is the Maid of Llanwellyn, who smiles upon me.

But Baillie's reshaping of these stanzas meant that the poem was not published until the second volume of Thomson's *Collection of Welsh Airs* came out in 1811.

After the publication of Baillie's 'O welcome bat and owlet gray' and 'The Black Cock' in Thomson's *Collection of Welsh Airs*, 1, in 1809, Thomson sent Baillie a present of an Indian shawl with a request that she write words for two Irish airs to which she agreed to 'some time hence try to find words for'.[35] On 8 May 1810, she sent him 'His boat comes on the sunny tide' and 'Come form we round a cheerful ring', which Thomson found little fault with and subsequently published in *A Collection of Irish Airs*, 1 (1814).

Thomson seemed to think that the more contributions he had from Baillie, the more his collections of Welsh, Irish and Scottish songs would sell. But perhaps Baillie found it almost impossible to alter her style to please Thomson and this difficulty accounted for her claim that she disliked writing poems that were to be set to music:

> I have frequently told you that I have no pleasure in writing Songs, and I am certainly not much in the mood for it at present; and moreover I do not believe the Work will be one bit better received by the public for having a greater or less proportion of the songs written by one person rather than another, yet that we may part in charity with one another at the end of it, if you will send me two of your airs I shall find words for them as well as I can.[36]

Baillie wrote these poems with some difficulty: 'I hoped to have sent them ["The morning air plays on my face . . ." and "The harper, who sat on his low mossy seat"] to you sooner, but it was not till the other morning that I could find quiet leisure to write anything, and I always like to let such things lie by me a day or two after they are written before I write out the clear copy . . .'[37] Thomson asked her to make minor emendations in these poems to which she agreed.

In relation to her writing of poems in Scots English, Baillie described to Thomson her difficulties, particularly in regard to the spelling of oral 'Scotch' words,

> The old, best set of the tune [for 'The Gowan glitters on the Sward'] indeed, if I may venture to say to you, is nothing better than an old *drunt* [a plaint], but as such I have a good will to it. Being Scotch music I have written Scotch words for it; not the old Scotch, but such Scotch as is still

spoken in the country. I hope you will not think it very bad; and as I don't very well know how to spell the Scotch words, I shall be obliged to you if you will have the goodness to correct the spelling.[38]

This West Mid Scots dialect was usually an oral language rather than a written one, which partly accounts for Baillie's problem in spelling these dialect words. Both Baillie and Thomson consulted John Jamieson's *Etymological Dictionary of the Scottish Language* (1808), a work which reflected the fact that by the end of the eighteenth century, modern Scots English had come to be seen by many Scots as an intrinsic expression of their own distinctive character as a people.

Despite Baillie's seeming deference to Thomson's editorial skills, at least in the initial stages of their contributor–editor relationship, she did not always agree to his editorial demands, but insisted on her right to have her words – whether Scots English or standard English – printed as she wished them to appear in his collections of songs.

In 1840, when Baillie had many of her poems from her anonymous volume of *Poems* reprinted in *Fugitive Verses*, she also included in this work three Scots English poems that Thomson asked in 1841 if he could reprint in his next edition of his six-volume *Collection of the Songs of Burns, Sir Walter Scott, Bart, and other Eminent Lyric Poets* (1841). Baillie responded,

> As to my three amended Scottish songs, 'Willie was a Wanton Wag' ['The Merry Bachelor'], 'Fee him, father, fee him', and 'Wi' lang-legged Tam the bruise I tried' ['My Nanny O'], you are heartily welcome to put them into your next publication of Scotch music. I shall be pleased to see them there; and you have no leave to ask any Bookseller, for they are entirely my own property. 'Fee him' I wrote for Miss Head of Ashfield Devonshire, who has a delightful voice and taste in music and gave her the MS copy many years ago, and it has been sung I believe by no one else.[39]

Margaret Carhart reports that Robert Burns admired the humour in Baillie's version of 'Fee him, father, fee him',[40] a fact which indicates that this 'amended Scotch song' dates back to at least 1796, the year of Burns's death. In 1802, Thomson had already printed 'Fee him, father, fee him' as an anonymous poem in *Fifty Scottish Songs with Symphonies and Accompaniments Wholly by Haydn*, vol. 3, but now he wished to reprint it with its correct attribution to Baillie. Baillie, despite her self-deprecation, was like Robert Burns an adept recaster of traditional Scottish songs long before Thomson commissioned her after Burns's death.

Baillie was also determined to have her own wishes adhered to in relation to the air that accompanied her words in 'Wi' lang-legged Tam the bruise I tried'. She informed Thomson,

I . . . thank you for the pains you are willing to take in favour of Lang-legged Tam ['My Nanny O'], but I should not like to have him joined to any other music than the old air of my Nanny O. It is one of those Scotch airs that may be made plaintive or joyous as you choose to sing or to play them: my song was intended to be in the last character, and Burns or Percy [Percy's *Reliques*] having written words for it, suited to the former, is a matter of no importance in itself; though I readily agree that there would be a confusion and waywardness in its appearing in its joyous mood in your last volume when it has keen melancholy and sentiment in the first. We shall, therefore, if you please think no more about it.[41]

Baillie, after receiving the approbation of the *Eclectic Magazine*, whose reviewer described her Scottish songs as 'only inferior to those of Burns . . . and quite equal to those of Sir W. Scott and Campbell',[42] seems to have gained more confidence in herself as a song-writer. To Thomson, she places herself on a level with Burns in relation to the adaptation and com-position of traditional Scottish songs. She also identifies a difference between her own adaptations of Scottish songs and those of Burns: Burns's songs tend to be 'plaintive' and hers are 'joyous' in words and mood.

This difference can be seen in their two different versions of 'A Weary Pund of Tow'. In both versions, the husband of the main protagonist of the poem narrates the story, but in Burns's poem, the unloving couple are intolerant of each other; the wife reduces her husband's 'gude' 'stane o' lint' to one 'poor pund o' tow' and then drowns in alcohol both her ill-feelings about spinning it and the flax itself. Her husband's remonstration leads to violence of a knockabout kind, 'She took her rock, and wi' a knock, / She brak it o'er my pow'. When, however, his wife dies – 'Gaed foremost o'er the knowe' – he vows to hang himself with flax before he weds 'anither jad'. James Kinsley comments that 'Burns's starting-point for this song was a graceless ditty in *The Charmer*, 1, p. 339 (1782), and other song-books. He has transformed this into a neat and witty domestic comedy'.[43]

Baillie might have based her 'The Weary Pund of Tow' on a version other than Burns's, or she might have invented this tale herself: Baillie focuses more sympathetically on the young wife, who is so busy gossiping, attending fairs and 'preachings', and dancing 'on the green' that she has no time to weave her 'pund of tow' [pound of flax]. The narrator is the young wife's husband whose affection for her will tolerate even his going 'sark-less' to his 'grave'.

Although both Burns and Baillie, in their respective versions of 'A Weary Pund o' Tow', rely for their comedy on their representations of the ill-done-by husband, Baillie's narrator is more tolerant of women's vices than is Burns's. In this instance, the difference between the two poems lies not in lewdness or its absence, but in Baillie's lighthearted tolerance of woman's peccadilloes.

Thomson also invited her to write a new version of 'The Wee Pickle Tow', but Baillie, who was then eighty, declined:

> I am pleased that you should still suppose I have spirit enough to deal with your Auld Wife and her wee pickle tow, but I do not feel that I have; the air is an excellent one, but who could give the proper alteration of the words better than Sir Adam [Fergusson] himself? Let *him* take it in hand . . .[44]

Despite her refusal, the idea must have taken her fancy, because 'New Words to the Old Scotch Air of "The Wee Pickle Tow"' appears in her collected *Dramatic and Poetical Works* (1851), but not in any of Thomson's collections of songs. In this song, the young girl's 'rock' [distaff with flax attached] with which she is spinning 'took a low', which means literally 'caught alight' or 'showed radiance as of fire' or, figuratively, 'fell into a state of ardour or excitement or a blaze of feeling'. The remainder of the poem centres on a play on the word 'low', with the young woman comically implying that the 'rock' took fire because of her thwarted sexual passion for her lover:

> They'll say I was doited, they'll say I was fou'
> They'll say I was dowie, and Robin untrue,
> They'll say in the fire some love-pouther I threw,
> And that made the ill beginning o't.

Baillie thus satirizes society's lack of recognition that spirited young women might need more than the occupation of spinning for the expression of their youthful 'fire'.

Baillie's voice in these poems in Scots English is distinctive in that she usually portrays her male protagonist as at a disadvantage in relation to a woman or to women, whom she generally represents in a sympathetic light. The anti-hero in 'Tam o' the Lin', for example, fades away to die in the heartbroken manner that is usually attributed to women. In 'Hooly and Fairly', the character of the lazy wife is presented more sympathetically than the figure of the suffering husband, who – as in Baillie's version of 'The Weary Pund of Tow' – is the naive narrator whom the audience laughs at rather than with.

Baillie's sympathetic approach to women characters in these Scots English and in her Irish and Welsh poems is noticeable also in her comic poem, 'It was on a morn when we were thrang'. This poem was commissioned for *The Harp of Caledonia* (1819) by John Struthers, the cobbler turned editor whom the Baillies had helped. This poem in Scots English employs the ambiguities of Scots words such as 'tight' in order to satirize effectively an ageing landlord's behaviour towards women.

In the composition of her earlier poems that she published in 1790, however, Baillie wrote in standard English enriched with a few lexical and structural features from modern (post-1700) Scots English. In *A Winter Day*, for example, she describes the approach of morning:

> For now the morning vapour, red and grumly,
> Rests heavy on the hills; and o'er the heavens
> Wide spreading forth in lighter gradual shades,
> Just faintly colours the pale muddy sky. (ll. 69-72)

This description of the sun-coloured mist which spreads 'faintly' into the 'pale muddy sky' gives a vivid pictorial image of a northern dawn sky in winter. She eschews the use of elaborate poetic diction and she draws on epithets from the language of the 'common people' as well as creating her own plain expression.

When Baillie came to revise 'A Winter Day' and 'A Summer Day' for reprinting fifty years later, she deleted a few Scotticisms, such as the word, 'grumly', which she replaced with 'dismal', or 'knotted shoes', which she replaced with 'studded shoes'. She also revised selected sections, particularly those in which she attempted to describe sublimity in the natural world; for example, her description of the winter dawn becomes more mannered and less direct in her 1840 version:

> The morning vapour rests upon the heights,
> Lurid and red, while growing gradual shades
> Of pale and sickly light spread o'er the sky.[45]

In the later version, 'heights', a more abstract term, is substituted for 'hills'; the sunlight is exaggerated as 'lurid and red', rather than merely 'red' in the early version; and 'growing gradual shades of pale and sickly light' replaces the more deft phrasing of 'faintly colours the pale muddy sky'. The concision and simplicity of diction which is notable in her 1790 versions of these blank verse poems is thus diluted with the effect of making the expression of these poems more elevated and less authentic. She also introduced a passage about the historical habit of evening religious worship among these smallholding families, which, in her 1840 note to this poem, she terms 'a great omission for which I justly take shame to myself'.[46] By then Baillie was seventy-eight, and had become more conscious of theology[47] as well as of religious life. It is in the early versions of these two long poems, and in her other similarly lively poems such as 'A Disappointment' and 'A Reverie', that Baillie uses standard English with an admixture of scattered Scotticisms so as to create original poems which are as evocative and vivid as her songs in Scots English are.

Just as Wordsworth, despite his avowed intention of writing poems 'in a selection of language really used by men',[48] did not employ the native speech of Northumbrians in his composition of ballads such as 'Goody Blake and Harry Gill' and 'The Idiot Boy', so Baillie before him had not used in her *Poems* (1790) variations of the Scots English that she had heard around her in Lanarkshire. Instead she composed a plain poetic language for her mainly London audience that suggested the rural environment that she attempted to recreate. In imagining the thoughts and speech of the anti-hero of 'A Disappointment', she employed colloquial language such as 'the hateful clown', 'grizzly suitors' and 'the black fiend may take them all for me!' rather than attempting to recreate the Scots English in which this male character might actually have spoken. Her projected audience was mainly the urban inhabitants of London who could not be expected to follow Scots English. She reserved the use of Scots English for her poems that were to be set for singing to traditional Scottish airs.

Content and form in Joanna Baillie's poems

In this selection, the first two poems – 'A Winter Day' and 'A Summer Day' – should be read in tandem since there are both contrasts and linkages between the themes and imagery of each. Through the use of a covert narrator, the differences between the seasons are highlighted, and, at the same time, a social commentary is adumbrated in relation to some aspects of eighteenth-century life.

In both poems, family life and rural surroundings are evoked in detail and celebrated with greater realism and less mawkishness than in Burns's 'The Cotter's Saturday Night' (1785-6). Moreover, unlike Burns, Baillie uses the more natural rhythms of blank verse rather than the Spenserian stanza, which had become associated – through Shenstone and Beattie – with supposedly rustic themes. The difficulties of the domestic and economic circumstances of the yeomanry are described in detail by Baillie, unlike some of the distancing from the subject matter that is apparent in some of the blank verse poems of another of her compatriots, James Thomson. In his poem 'Winter' (1726), for example, Thomson describes 'the cottage-swain' who

> Hangs o'er th'enlivening blaze and, taleful, there
> Recounts his simple frolic; much he talks
> And much he laughs, nor recks the storm that blows
> Without, and rattles on his humble roof.[49]

Thomson's 'swain' seems more generalized and less distinctive than Baillie's 'hind' whom she characterizes in detail in 'A Winter Day'.

In Baillie's poem, the narrator concentrates on the smallholding yeoman farmer and his family, showing how he is slow to get up in the cold darkness, wryly wishing that he 'were a lord, / That he might lie a-bed'. The family's breakfast is the porridge that was usual in cottage meals of that time; the children play on snow and ice; a black cock is shot wantonly by a fowler; and a mendicant soldier is given a bed for the night. In 'A Summer Day', the narrator centres on a labourer, who, in the first light of morning 'quits his easy bed' and 'with good will begins his daily work' of digging with spade and hoe. Children play in the early sunshine, and a housewife separates curd and whey in making cheese. At noon, when 'all the freshness of the morn is fled', the mowing with scythes commences and everyone joins in – 'old and young, the weak and strong' – to stack the new-mown hay in a haystack. Children bring lunch for a meal in the field; this is followed by a siesta, then more haying. At sundown everyone returns to the village, where young men and women flirt, and children play. A pedlar arrives and the villagers are attracted to his flashy wares. The poem concludes with an image of sleep for everyone except for a frustrated lover who lurks in a copse awaiting 'his darling maid'.

The main difference between Baillie's two season poems lies in their tone and mood. In 'A Winter Day', a sense of foreboding and desolation is created through the use of adjectives in phrases such as 'bleak and dreary' and 'the rugged face of scowling winter'. In 'A Summer Day', a mood of joyful labour and fulfilment is created in phrases such as 'the cheerful voice of industry' and 'thus do they jest, and laugh away their toil'. In 'A Winter Day', the imagery is dominated by violence, such as the shooting of the cock, and the soldier's tales. In 'A Summer Day', the imagery is connected with ripeness and sexuality; for example, the housewife is assisted in making cheese by 'her brown dimpled maid, with tucked-up sleeve, / And swelling arm' and the haymaking is accompanied by laughter and flirtation.[50]

Inherent in Baillie's celebrations of the pastoral is a critique of the artificiality of town life with its incessant quest for pleasure in contrast with the 'natural' existence of the rural yeomanry with their balance between physical labour and calm relaxation. In 'A Winter Day', after listening to 'tales of war and blood', the villagers retire not 'torn with vexing cares, / Nor dancing with the unequal beat of pleasure'. The main enemy that the yeoman fears is an accepted fact of Nature – storms, which 'break in dreadful bellowings o'er his head'. Those who are unluckily excluded from a family circle are represented as pitiable. The mendicant ex-soldier, for instance, who is taken in for the night by the yeoman farmer, is not easily rehabilitated into civilian society:

> They gaze upon him,
> And almost weep to see the man so poor,
> So bent and feeble, helpless and forlorn,
> That oft has stood undaunted in the battle
> Whilst thundering cannons shook the quaking earth,
> And showering bullets hissed around his head.

This representation of battle contrasts dramatically with the rural haven in which the farming community lives, and alludes indirectly to the period between 1775 and 1783 during which Britain was at war with France and Spain as well as with the American colonists.

Baillie's ability to use various poetic forms which express what she has observed in the Scottish rural community is shown in her major narrative poems – 'A Disappointment' and 'A Reverie' – in which she develops characterization through the use of internal monologues. These early poems are forerunners to her blank verse dramas and in her 'Introductory Discourse' to *A Series of Plays* (1798), Baillie outlines her approach to the representation of character:

> The highest pleasures we receive from poetry . . . are derived from the sympathetic interest we all take in beings like ourselves; and I will even venture to say, that were the grandest scenes which can enter into the imagination of man presented to our view and all reference to man completely shut off from our thoughts, the objects that composed it would convey to our minds little better than dry ideas of magnitude, colour, and form; and the remembrance of them would rest upon our minds like the measurement and distances of the planets.[51]

In these lines, Baillie dismisses neo-classical conventions of pastoral artifice and stock reflection on manners.

By 1790, she had already attempted to put her maxims about the necessity for realistic characterization into practice in a narrative poem, 'A Disappointment', about the reactions of a jilted lover, William, who has been spurned because he lacks wealth. William's sexual frustration and social humiliation are expressed through his first-person venting of his sarcastic envy of his successful rival, whose looks do not match his material possessions:

> 'Ay, lucky churl! No store thy cottage lacks,
> But round thy barn thick stand the sheltered stacks.
> But did such features coarse my visage grace,
> I'd never budge the bonnet from my face.'

The poem concludes with the third-person narrator giving a humorous account of William kicking his dog, Tray: 'Up jumped the kindly beast his hand to lick, / And, for his pains, received an angry kick'.

Through a combination of indirect narration and internal monologue, marriage mores among the Scottish smallholders and villagers are universalized and satirized. In the following excerpt, for example, the village reaction to the passing wedding-party is particularized:

> Each village wag with eye of roguish cast,
> Some maiden jogs and vents the ready jest;
> While village toasts the passing belles deride,
> And sober matrons marvel at their pride.

This description is humorously ironic in its reference to 'village toasts' who deride 'passing belles' – those women who are popular with men. These lines send up the vanity and social self-importance of the individuals in the village throng. Baillie's realistic yet sympathetic tale of spurned love is thus counterpointed by satiric comments. Although Baillie's form is that of conventional heroic couplets, her use of everyday descriptive language and internal monologue were innovatory in 1790 and are still fresh today.

Similarly, in 'A Reverie', the male protagonist, Robin, projects on to Nelly his dreams of a settled domestic life. Baillie uses the third person to set the scene, which is succeeded by an internal monologue from Robin, who fantasizes about his prospective 'help-mate' even though he has no 'dower, but love' to offer her. He meditates on whether Nelly has yet discovered that he admires her:

> 'I pulled the blossoms from the bending tree,
> And some to Susan gave, and some to thee;
> Thine were the best, and well thy smiling eye
> The difference marked, and guessed the reason why.'

Baillie then reverts from first-person monologue to direct narration in describing her anti-hero, Robin, impulsively chasing after Nelly who is seated on a passing haywain. The conclusion to this 'love story' is open-ended and non-moralistic: 'tracts of trodden grain, and sidelong hay, / And broken hedge-flowers sweet, mark his impetuous way'. The reader is left to guess at Robin's chances at attaining his 'love'. This poem thus satirizes masculine illusions before marriage, a satiric note which is reflected in the title, which in Scots English means 'raving nonsense, foolish talk'.

In 'A Lamentation', Baillie again combines the devices of direct narration and internal monologue. The chief protagonist, Basil, mourns the loss of his beloved Mary at her tombstone in the church graveyard. Basil cries out his woes until the church-bell rings, disturbing the screech-owl and the bat. The narrator with grim humour shows Basil reacting to this disturbance by thinking that the noises emanate from the uncanny. In fact, he thinks that the white tombstones which surround him are ghosts: 'Dim thro' the gloom they showed their forms unknown'. He is terrified, and 'with knocking limbs, and quickened breath, / His footstep urges from the place of death'. Baillie here uses incidents in the ordinary world in order to dramatize a psychological change of mood in her subject. In 'A Disappointment', 'A Reverie' and 'A Lamentation', Baillie successfully creates character, mood, and storyline which, apart from her use of heroic couplets, are comparable to Burns's satires such as 'Tam o' Shanter' and Wordsworth's later deconstructions of superstition in ballads such as 'Goody Blake and Harry Gill'.

Many readers might now find Baillie's addresses to her sister, Agnes, and her friend, Mrs Sarah Siddons, the actress, of interest because these occasional poems have an authentic expression and interesting content. In 'Lines to Agnes Baillie on her Birthday', Baillie describes their early childhood experience in the valley of the River Clyde: 'Then every butterfly that crossed our view / With joyful shout was greeted as it flew . . .' Her recapitulation of her childhood vividly recalls their enjoyment of the natural world in a way which anticipates George Eliot's later sequence of sonnets, *Brother and Sister* (1869), on that same theme.

Baillie's lyrics about relationships between adults and children reflect eighteenth-century interest in the psychological and moral development of children. These lyrics anticipate some of William Wordsworth's poems in that Baillie uses a then novel technique of employing disingenuous narrators whose stories can be reinterpreted by sophisticated readers; for example, in 'A Mother to Her Waking Infant', the narrator describes in minute detail the behaviour of a young baby as seen from a devoted mother's point of view. She muses over her baby's lack of physical coordination and inability to form words or even to express by gesture a sophisticated range of feelings:

> From thy poor tongue no accents come,
> Which can but curb thy toothless gum;
> Small understanding boasts thy face,
> Thy shapeless limbs nor step nor grace:
> A few short words thy feats may tell,
> And yet I love thee well.

In this lyric, which is composed of sestets of rhyming tetrameters which conclude with a trimeter, Baillie shows the play of feeling in a new mother in relation to her observation of her helpless baby. The poem, 'A Child to His Sick Grandfather', represents from the point of view of a devoted young grandson an old man who is on the threshold of death. These two poems reflect the development of an eighteenth-century enlightenment about the importance of early childhood experience, a notion which has persisted into twentieth-century ideologies about the psychology of childhood.[52]

Baillie and the Romantic canon

Readers in the field of British Romantic poetry have been generally encouraged by literary critics to revere the works of Blake, Burns, William Wordsworth, S. T. Coleridge, Byron, Keats, and Shelley. The poetry of John Clare is now often accepted as part of this 'canon' also. Some critics in the last ten years have attempted to renew readers' interest in women poets of the Romantic period, so that we now have available various anthologies of Romantic poetry which include a proportion of women poets or are devoted entirely to women poets.[53] Annotated editions of the collected poems of both Charlotte Smith and Anna Letitia Barbauld have also been brought out recently, but Joanna Baillie's lyric poetry has continued to be overlooked.[54]

Baillie's meditative lyrics on the nature of rural life, her dramatic poems on rural experiences, some of her poems about children, and her various songs show that as a poet she has a remarkable range of linguistic virtuosity. If we read her lyric poems with an open mind today, we cannot but admit that she should be accorded the same accolades that we give to the Scots English songs of Robert Burns and the meditative Nature poetry of William Wordsworth.

One argument against placing Baillie in the 'canon' with Wordsworth has been that she does not show the same interest in the psychology of feeling that he evinces in poems such as *The Prelude*. That argument seems inappropriate in the light of the range of poems in this selection. When assessing the aesthetic merit of individual poets we must look at what is unique and original in each author's work and not at what is similar in it to the work of some canonical poet. What Baillie does well is to write specifically about characters who are working people, whether in their authentic-sounding voices or in descriptions of their lives. Literary histories of the Romantic Period need to be revised in order to take into account Baillie's original *Poems* (1790) about rural people's lives, which predate Wordsworth's similar poems on that topic. No literary critic should claim, after reading this volume carefully, that Baillie's finest poems such as 'A Disappointment' or 'Fee him, father, fee him' are in any way inferior to – even if they are *different* from – Wordsworth's *Lyrical Ballads* (1798) or Burns's Scots English poems. In fact, readers will now be able to appreciate fully Baillie's authentic specificity in subject matter and style which place her lyric poetry at the centre of that late eighteenth-century literary and cultural movement that critics term 'Romanticism'.

Notes

1   Joanna Baillie, *Poems: Wherein it is Attempted to Describe Certain Views of Nature and Rustic Manners*, London, Joseph Johnson, 1790.

2   Joanna Baillie, *Fugitive Verses*, London, Edward Moxon, 1840.

3   Joanna Baillie, ed., *A Collection of Poems, Chiefly Manuscript, and from Living Authors*, London, Longman, Hurst, Rees, Orme, and Brown, 1823.

4   Joanna Baillie, *The Dramatic and Poetical Works*, London, Longman, Brown and Green and Longmans, 1851.

5   See, for example, Humphrey Milford, ed., *The Oxford Book of English Verse of the Romantic Period*, Oxford, Oxford University Press, 1928, reissued 1935.

6   George Watson, ed., *The Shorter New Cambridge Bibliography of English Literature*, Cambridge, Cambridge University Press, 1981.

7   Roger Lonsdale, *The New Oxford Book of Eighteenth-Century Verse*, Oxford, Oxford University Press, 1984, p. 855.

8   *Poems* (1790), facsimile repr., in *Revolution and Romanticism Series, 1789-1834*, Woodstock Books, Oxford and New York, 1994, p. 10.

9   For a discussion of 'orientalism' see, for example, Marilyn Butler, 'Orientalism', in David B. Pirie, ed., *The Penguin History of Literature*, Harmondsworth, Penguin, 1994, pp. 395-447; for exegeses of some of Baillie's narrative poems, see Amanda Gilroy, 'From Here to Alterity: The Geography of Femininity in the Poetry of Joanna Baillie', in *A History of Scottish Women's Writing*, ed. Douglas Gifford and Dorothy McMillan, Edinburgh, Edinburgh University Press, 1997, pp. 143-57.

10 See *Dictionary of National Biography*.

11 Letter to George Thomson, 12 March 1822, BL Add. MS. 35265, f. 108.

12 Margaret S. Carhart, *The Life and Work of Joanna Baillie*, London and New Haven, Yale University Press, 1923, pp. 3-12.

13 *The Monthly Review*, 6 (1791), pp. 266-9.

14 Marilyn Butler, *Romantics, Rebels and Reactionaries: English Literature and Its Background, 1760-1830*, Oxford, Oxford University Press, 1981, p. 58.

15 'Introductory Discourse', *A Series of Plays*, 1798, facsimile edn, 1990, p. 42.

16 Stuart Curran, 'Romantic Poetry: The "I" Altered', in *Romanticism and Feminism*, ed. Anne Mellor, Bloomington, Indiana University Press, 1988, p. 186. For subsequent critical discussion of Baillie's blank verse dramas, see, for example, Catherine B. Burroughs, 'English Romantic Women Writers and Theatre Theory: Joanna Baillie's Prefaces to the *Plays on the Passions*', in *Re-visioning Romanticism: British Women Writers, 1776-1837*, ed. Carol Shiner Wilson and Joel Haefner, Philadelphia, University of Pennsylvania Press, 1994, pp. 274-96; or Marjean D. Purinton, *Romantic Ideology Unmasked: The Mentally Constructed Tyrannies in*

Dramas of William Wordsworth, Lord Byron, Percy Shelley, and Joanna Baillie, Newark, Del., University of Delaware Press, 1994.

17 Joanna Baillie, *Recollections Written at the Request of Miss Berry*, London, Royal College of Surgeons Library, Hunter-Baillie Collection, vol. 2, no. 56, 1831.

18 *The New Oxford Book of Eighteenth-Century Verse*, p. 523, ll. 9-14.

19 *Ibid.* p. 601, ll. 41-4.

20 *Ibid.* p. 225, ll. 52-3.

21 George Crabbe, *Selected Poems*, ed. Gavin Edwards, Harmondsworth, Penguin, 1991, *The Village*, Book I, p. 8, ll. 170-80.

22 Jerome McGann argues that George Crabbe is not a 'romantic' writer: 'The contradictions of the period help to explain why some of its most impressive writing is not romantic writing. So far as poetry is concerned, Crabbe is the central instance' ('Introduction', *The New Oxford Book of Romantic Period Verse*, Oxford, Oxford University Press, 1993, p. xxii). But to write about ordinary or 'common' people in Wordsworth's case is seen to epitomize Romanticism.

23 Janice Patten demonstrates how Baillie, in her later three inaugural dramas, *A Series of Plays on the Passions* (1798), continues to pursue 'a new poetics which raises the importance of imagination to new heights, and dramatizes in beautiful natural language persons of "humble and lowly class" as they respond to "beauty", or labour under self-doubt, haunted by memories, often wandering alone in nature' ('Joanna Baillie, *A Series of Plays*', in *A Companion to British Romanticism*, ed. Duncan Wu, Oxford, Blackwell, 1998, p. 170).

24 'Introductory Discourse', *A Series of Plays*, 1798, see Appendix 1, p. 190.

25 George Crabbe contributed 'Hope and Memory' to her compilation of her contemporaries' poems, *A Collection of Poems* (1823), for which William Wordsworth, Robert Southey and Sir Walter Scott also wrote poems. See Baillie's letter to George Crabbe, 13 June 1822, in which she thanked him for sending her a revised manuscript copy of 'Hope and Memory' which she published in her *Collection of Poems* (1823), pp. 56-64. In her letter, Baillie expressed her gratitude at having 'such a name [Crabbe's] to grace my list of Poetical friends' (Brotherton Library, Leeds, MS Collection).

26 See *Correspondence between Joanna Baillie and Sir Walter Scott, 1809-1829*, National Library of Scotland, MSS 3876-3910.

27 Carhart, *The Life and Work of Joanna Baillie*, p. 168.

28 James Johnson, 'Preface', *The Scots Musical Museum*, 2, 1788, p. iii.

29 George Thomson, letter to Robert Burns, quoted in *The Poems and Songs of Robert Burns*, vol. 2, ed. James Kinsley, 1970, p. 990.

30 George Thomson, 'Preface', *Collection of the Songs of Burns, Sir Walter Scott, Bart, and other Eminent Lyric Poets Ancient and Modern United to the Select Melodies of Scotland, and of Ireland and Wales, with Symphonies and Accompaniments . . . by Pleyel, Haydn, Beethoven and Kozeluck*, 6 vols, London and Edinburgh, 1822.

31 Letter to George Thomson, 18 February 1804, BL Add. MS. 35263, fos. 217-20.

32 Letter to George Thomson, 17 January 1809, BL Add. MS. 35263, f. 304.

33 BL Add. MS. 35263, f. 222.

34 Letter to George Thomson, 27 April 1804, BL Add. MS. 35263, f. 221.

35 Letter to George Thomson, 6 January 1810, BL Add. MS. 35263, f. 312.

36 Letter to George Thomson, 1 February 1813, BL Add. MS. 35264, f. 80.

37 Letter to George Thomson, 19 April 1813, BL Add. MS. 35264, f. 98.

38 Letter to George Thomson, 16 December 1811, BL Add. MS. 35264, f. 58.

39 Letter to George Thomson, 1 May 1841, BL Add. MS. 35265, f. 286.

40 Carhart, *The Life and Work of Joanna Baillie*, p. 168.

41 Letter to George Thomson, 10 May 1841, BL Add. MS. 35265, fos. 290-1.

42 *Eclectic Magazine*, N. S., vol. 1, p. 420.

43 James Kinsley, ed., *The Poems of Robert Burns*, vol. 2, pp. 622-3.

44 Letter to George Thomson, 30 March 1842, BL Add. MS. 35265, f. 320.

45 See my anthology, *Women Romantic Poets, 1785-1832* (1992, new edn 1994), p. 45, ll. 69-71.

46 See notes on the poems, this volume p. 149.

47 Baillie had always attended church regularly, and in Hampstead she worshipped at both the High Anglican church (in whose churchyard she is buried) as well as the dissenters' Unitarian chapel at which Anna Barbauld's husband Rochemont Barbauld preached before he became insane. In 1831, Baillie published a pamphlet, *A View of the General Tenor of the New Testament regarding the Nature and Dignity of Jesus Christ* (London, Longman) about the nature and humanity of Jesus Christ. Subsequently, she engaged in a dispute on this subject with the Bishop of Salisbury. She then published their exchange of letters in her second edition (1838) of this pamphlet.

48 See William Wordsworth, 'Preface', *Poetical Works*, ed. Thomas Hutchinson, new edn, ed. Ernest de Selincourt, London, Oxford University Press, 1936, p. 734.

49 *The New Oxford Book of Eighteenth-Century Verse*, p. 182, ll. 128-32.

50 Cf. Isobel Armstrong's exegesis of Anna Barbauld's 'Inscription for an Ice-house' in which Armstrong reflects on Barbauld's 'feminine symbolism' in relation to 'generative excess' ('The Gush of the Feminine: How Can We Read Women's Poetry of the Romantic Period?' in *Romantic Women Writers: Voices and Counter-voices*, ed. Paula R. Feldman and Theresa M. Kelley, Hanover and London, University Press of New England, 1995, p. 19).

51 'Introductory Discourse', *A Series of Plays*, 1798, see Appendix 1, p. 191.

52 Cf. Jerome McGann in *The Poetics of Sensibility*, Oxford, Oxford University Press, 1996, relates 'A Mother to Her Waking Infant' to an emergent literary tradition of poetry of sentiment and sensibility, p. 70.

53 See, for example, Roger Lonsdale, *Eighteenth-Century Women Poets: An Oxford Anthology*, Oxford, Oxford University Press, 1989. My anthology, *Women Romantic Poets, 1785-1832: An Anthology*, Everyman/Dent, 1992; new edn, 1994, was the first of the anthologies devoted entirely to a selection of women poets of the Romantic period. Subsequently *The New Oxford Book of Romantic Period Verse*, ed. Jerome McGann, Oxford, Oxford University Press, 1993, which includes fourteen women poets; *Romantic Women Poets*, vol. 1, 1994, rev. 1998, and vol. 2, 1998, ed. Andrew Ashfield, Manchester, Manchester University Press; and *Romantic Women Poets: An Anthology*, ed. Duncan Wu, Oxford, Blackwell, 1996, have appeared.

54 See my bibliographical chapter, 'Women Poets of the Romantic Period', in *Literature of the Romantic Period: A Bibliographical Guide*, ed. Michael O'Neill, Oxford, Oxford University Press, 1998, pp. 181-91.

Note on the texts of the poems

Joanna Baillie's poems have been selected from her following works: *Poems: Wherein It Is Attempted to Describe Certain Views of Nature and Rustic Manners* (1790); *A Collection of Poems* (1823), edited by Joanna Baillie, which includes five of her own poems; *Fugitive Verses* (1840); and *The Dramatic and Poetical Works of Joanna Baillie* (1851). The text of the excerpt from *Introductory Discourse* (Appendix 1) comes from her *A Series of Plays, in which it is Attempted to Delineate the Strong Passions of the Mind*, 3 vols, 1798-1812; and the text of *Preface* (Appendix 2) comes from *Fugitive Verses* (1840).

The poems in standard English or English with a few Scots English words, have been reprinted here in a modernized form, with unnecessary initial capital letters and italicized words deleted. Many contractions have also been expanded because, although such contractions were common in late eighteenth-century poetry, they are usually now not metrically necessary.

The poems in Scots English have not been modernized in this manner because recent Scots English spelling systems, such as the Makars Club's *Scots Style Sheet* (1947), have not become established and Baillie's Scots English spelling is therefore just as accessible as any other Scots English system is to readers today. Scots English words are glossed in the notes on the poems.

The poems are printed in chronological order of the date of publication, where known; otherwise the poems are printed in the order in which Joanna Baillie arranged them respectively in her three volumes cited above. The date of the first publication is given in the notes on the poems.

The poems

1 *A Farm in Lanarkshire* by Alexander Naysmith (1758–1840)

shows the type of landscape described by Joanna Baillie in her two linked poems,
A Winter Day and *A Summer Day*

A WINTER DAY

The cock, warm roosting 'midst his feathered dames,
Now lifts his beak and snuffs the morning air,
Stretches his neck and claps his heavy wings,
Gives three hoarse crows, and glad his task is done;
Low, chuckling, turns himself upon the roost,
Then nestles down again amongst his mates.
The labouring hind, who on his bed of straw,
Beneath his home-made coverings, coarse, but warm,
Locked in the kindly arms of her who spun them,
Dreams of the gain that next year's crop should bring;   10
Or at some fair disposing of his wool,
Or by some lucky and unlooked-for bargain,
Fills his skin purse with heaps of tempting gold,
Now wakes from sleep at the unwelcome call,
And finds himself but just the same poor man
As when he went to rest. –
He hears the blast against his window beat,
And wishes to himself he were a lord,
That he might lie abed. –
He rubs his eyes, and stretches out his arms;   20
Heigh ho! heigh ho! he drawls with gaping mouth,
Then most unwillingly creeps out of bed,
And without looking-glass puts on his clothes.
With rueful face he blows the smothered fire,
And lights his candle at the reddening coal;
First sees that all be right amongst his cattle,
Then hies him to the barn with heavy tread,
Printing his footsteps on the new fallen snow.
From out the heap of corn he pulls his sheaves
Dislodging the poor redbreast from his shelter,   30
Where all the livelong night he slept secure;
But now affrighted, with uncertain flight
He flutters round the walls, to seek some hole,
At which he may escape out to the frost.
And now the flail, high whirling o'er his head,
Descends with force upon the jumping sheave,
Whilst every rugged wall, and neighbouring cot
Re-echoes back the noise of his strokes.

The family cares call next upon the wife
To quit her mean but comfortable bed.   40
And first she stirs the fire, and blows the flame,
Then from her heap of sticks, for winter stored,
An armful brings; loud crackling as they burn,
Thick fly the red sparks upward to the roof,
While slowly mounts the smoke in wreathy clouds.
On goes the seething pot with morning cheer,
For which some little wishful hearts await,
Who, peeping from the bedclothes, spy, well-pleased,
The cheery light that blazes on the wall,
And bawl for leave to rise. –   50
Their busy mother knows not where to turn,
Her morning work comes now so thick upon her.
One she must help to tie his little coat,
Unpin his cap, and seek another's shoe.
When all is o'er, out to the door they run,
With new combed sleeky hair, and glistening cheeks,
Each with some little project in his head.
One on the ice must try his new soled shoes:
To view his well-set trap another hies,
In hopes to find some poor unwary bird   60
(No worthless prize) entangled in his snare;
Whilst one, less active, with round rosy face,
Spreads out his purple fingers to the fire,
And peeps, most wishfully, into the pot.

       But let us leave the warm and cheerful house,
To view the bleak and dreary scene without,
And mark the dawning of a winter day.
For now the morning vapour, red and grumly,
Rests heavy on the hills; and o'er the heavens
Wide spreading forth in lighter gradual shades,   70
Just faintly colours the pale muddy sky.
Then slowly from behind the southern hills,
Enlarged and ruddy looks the rising sun,
Shooting his beams askance the hoary waste,
Which gild the brow of every swelling height,
And deepen every valley with a shade.
The crusted window of each scattered cot,
The icicles that fringe the thatched roof,

The new swept slide upon the frozen pool,
All lightly glance, new kindled with his rays;   80
And e'en the rugged face of scowling Winter
Looks somewhat gay. But for a little while
He lifts his glory o'er the brightening earth,
Then hides his head behind a misty cloud.

     The birds now quit their holes and lurking sheds,
Most mute and melancholy, where thro' night
All nestling close to keep each other warm,
In downy sleep they had forgot their hardships;
But not to chant and carol in the air,
Or lightly swing upon some waving bough,   90
And merrily return each other's notes;
No; silently they hop from bush to bush,
Yet find no seeds to stop their craving want,
Then bend their flight to the low smoking cot,
Chirp on the roof, or at the window peck,
To tell their wants to those who lodge within.
The poor lank hare flies homeward to his den,
But little burthened with his nightly meal
Of withered greens grubbed from the farmer's garden;
A poor and scanty portion snatched in fear;   100
And fearful creatures, forced abroad by want,
Are now to every enemy a prey.

     The husbandman lays by his heavy flail,
And to the house returns, where on him wait
His smoking breakfast and impatient children;
Who, spoon in hand, and longing to begin,
Towards the door cast many a weary look
To see their dad come in. –
Then round they sit, a cheerful company,
All eagerly begin, and with heaped spoons   110
Besmear from ear to ear their rosy cheeks.
The faithful dog stands by his master's side
Wagging his tail, and looking in his face;
While humble puss pays court to all around,
And purs and rubs them with her furry sides;
Nor goes this little flattery unrewarded.
But the laborious sit not long at table;

The grateful father lifts his eyes to heaven
To bless his God, whose ever bounteous hand
Him and his little ones doth daily feed;   120
Then rises satisfied to work again.

      The cheerful rousing noise of industry
Is heard, with varied sounds, thro' all the village.
The humming wheel, the thrifty housewife's tongue,
Who scolds to keep her maidens at their work,
Rough grating cards, and voice of squalling children
Issue from every house. –
But, hark! – the sportsman from the neighbouring hedge
His thunder sends! – loud barks each village cur;
Up from her wheel each curious maiden starts,   130
And hastens to the door, whilst matrons chide,
Yet run to look themselves, in spite of thrift,
And all the little town is in a stir.

      Strutting before, the cock leads forth his train,
And, chuckling near the barn among the straw,
Reminds the farmer of his morning's service;
His grateful master throws a liberal handful;
They flock about it, whilst the hungry sparrows
Perched on the roof, look down with envious eye,
Then, aiming well, amidst the feeders light,   140
And seize upon the feast with greedy bill,
Till angry partlets peck them off the field.
But at a distance, on the leafless tree,
All woebegone, the lonely blackbird sits;
The cold north wind ruffles his glossy feathers;
Full oft he looks, but dare not make approach;
Then turns his yellow bill to peck his side,
And claps his wings close to his sharpened breast.
The wandering fowler, from behind the hedge,
Fastens his eye upon him, points his gun,   150
And firing wantonly as at a mark,
E'en lays him low in that same cheerful spot
Which oft hath echoed with his evening's song.

      The day now at its height, the pent-up kine
Are driven from their stalls to take the air.

How stupidly they stare! And feel how strange!
They open wide their smoking mouths to low,
But scarcely can their feeble sound be heard;
They turn and lick themselves, and step by step
Move dull and heavy to their stalls again.   160
In scattered groups the little idle boys
With purple fingers, moulding in the snow
Their icy ammunition, pant for war;
And, drawing up in opposite array,
Send forth a mighty shower of well-aimed balls,
Whilst little heroes try their growing strength,
And burn to beat the enemy off the field.
Or on the well-worn ice in eager throngs,
Aiming their race, shoot rapidly along,
Trip up each other's heels, and on the surface   170
With knotted shoes, draw many a chalky line.
Untired of play, they never cease their sport
Till the faint sun has almost run his course,
And threatening clouds, slow rising from the north,
Spread grumly darkness o'er the face of heaven;
Then, by degrees, they scatter to their homes,
With many a broken head and bloody nose,
To claim their mothers' pity, who, most skilful,
Cures all their troubles with a bit of bread.

      The night comes on apace –   180
Chill blows the blast, and drives the snow in wreaths.
Now every creature looks around for shelter,
And, whether man or beast, all move alike
Towards their several homes; and happy they
Who have a house to screen them from the cold!
Lo, o'er the frost a reverend form advances!
His hair white as the snow on which he treads,
His forehead marked with many a careworn furrow,
Whose feeble body, bending o'er a staff,
Still shows that once it was the seat of strength,   190
Tho' now it shakes like some old ruined tower.
Clothed indeed, but not disgraced with rags,
He still maintains that decent dignity
Which well becomes those who have served their country.
With tottering steps he to the cottage moves:

The wife within, who hears his hollow cough,
And pattering of his stick upon the threshold,
Sends out her little boy to see who's there.
The child looks up to view the stranger's face,
And seeing it enlightened with a smile,   200
Holds out his little hand to lead him in.
Roused from her work, the mother turns her head,
And sees them, not ill-pleased. –
The stranger whines not with a piteous tale,
But only asks a little, to relieve
A poor old soldier's wants. –
The gentle matron brings the ready chair,
And bids him sit, to rest his wearied limbs,
And warm himself before her blazing fire.
The children, full of curiosity,   210
Flock round, and with their fingers in their mouths,
Stand staring at him; whilst the stranger, pleased,
Takes up the youngest boy upon his knee.
Proud of its seat, it wags its little feet,
And prates, and laughs, and plays with his white locks.
But soon the soldier's face lays off its smiles;
His thoughtful mind is turned on other days,
When his own boys were wont to play around him,
Who now lie distant from their native land
In honourable, but untimely graves.   220
He feels how helpless and forlorn he is,
And bitter tears gush from his dim-worn eyes.
His toilsome daily labour at an end,
In comes the wearied master of the house,
And marks with satisfaction his old guest,
With all his children round. –
His honest heart is filled with manly kindness;
He bids him stay, and share their homely meal,
And take with them his quarters for the night.
The weary wanderer thankfully accepts,   230
And, seated with the cheerful family,
Around the plain but hospitable board,
Forgets the many hardships he has passed.

        When all are satisfied, about the fire
They draw their seats, and form a cheerful ring.

The thrifty housewife turns her spinning wheel;
The husband, useful even in his rest,
A little basket weaves of willow twigs,
To bear her eggs to town on market days;
And work but serves to enliven conversation.   240
Some idle neighbours now come straggling in,
Draw round their chairs, and widen out the circle.
Without a glass the tale and jest go round;
And everyone, in his own native way,
Does what he can to cheer the merry group.
Each tells some little story of himself,
That constant subject upon which mankind,
Whether in court or country, love to dwell.
How at a fair he saved a simple clown
From being tricked in buying of a cow;   250
Or laid a bet upon his horse's head
Against his neighbour's, bought for twice his price,
Which failed not to repay his better skill:
Or on a harvest day, bound in an hour
More sheaves of corn than any of his fellows,
Tho' ne'er so keen, could do in twice the time.
But chief the landlord, at his own fireside,
Doth claim the right of being listened to;
Nor dares a little bawling tongue be heard,
Tho' but in play, to break upon his story.   260
The children sit and listen with the rest;
And should the youngest raise its little voice,
The careful mother, ever on the watch,
And always pleased with what her husband says,
Gives it a gentle tap upon the fingers,
Or stops its ill-timed prattle with a kiss.
The soldier next, but not unasked, begins,
And tells in better speech what he has seen;
Making his simple audience to shrink
With tales of war and blood. They gaze upon him,   270
And almost weep to see the man so poor,
So bent and feeble, helpless and forlorn,
That oft has stood undaunted in the battle
Whilst thundering cannons shook the quaking earth,
And showering bullets hissed around his head.
With little care they pass away the night,

Till time draws on when they should go to bed;
Then all break up, and each retires to rest
With peaceful mind, nor torn with vexing cares,
Nor dancing with the unequal beat of pleasure.   280

      But long accustomed to observe the weather,
The labourer cannot lay him down in peace
Till he has looked to mark what bodes the night.
He turns the heavy door, thrusts out his head,
Sees wreaths of snow heaped up on every side,
And black and grumly all above his head,
Save when a red gleam shoots along the waste
To make the gloomy night more terrible.
Loud blows the northern blast –
He hears it hollow grumbling from afar,   290
Then, gathering strength, roll on with doubled might,
And break in dreadful bellowings o'er his head;
Like pithless saplings bend the vexed trees,
And their wide branches crack. He shuts the door,
And, thankful for the roof that covers him,
Hies him to bed.

A SUMMER DAY

The dark-blue clouds of night in dusky lines,
Drawn wide and streaky o'er the purer sky,
Wear faint the morning purple on their skirts.
The stars that full and bright shone in the west
But dimly twinkle to the steadfast eye;
And seen, and vanishing, and seen again,
Like dying tapers smothering in their sockets,
Appear at last shut from the face of heaven;
Whilst every lesser flame which shone by night,
The flashy meteor from the opening cloud,   10
That shoots full oft across the dusky sky;
Or wandering fire which looks across the marsh,
Beaming like candle in a lonely cot,

2 *Bothwell Bridge from Bothwell Park, Lanarkshire* by Patrick Gibson (1782–1829)

depicts the countryside in which Joanna Baillie spent her early years and on which
she drew in writing *Poems* (1790)

To cheer the hopes of the benighted traveller,
Till swifter than the very change of thought,
It shifts from place to place, escapes his glance,
And makes him wondering rub his doubtful eyes;
Or humble glow-worm, or the silver moth,
Which cast a feeble glimmering o'er the green,
All die away. –   20
For now the sun, slow moving in his grandeur,
Above the eastern mountains lifts his head.
The webs of dew spread o'er the hoary lawn,
The smooth clear bosom of the settled pool,
The polished ploughshare on the distant field,
Catch fire from him, and dart their new got beams
Upon the dazzled eye.

        The new-waked birds upon the branches hop,
Peck their soft down, and bristle out their feathers;
Then stretch their throats and tune their morning song;   30
Whilst stately crows, high swinging o'er their heads,
Upon the topmost boughs, in lordly pride,
Mix their hoarse croaking with the linnet's note;
Till gathered closer in a sable band,
They take their flight to seek their daily food.
The village labourer, with careful mind,
As soon as doth the morning light appear,
Opens his eyes with the first darting ray
That pierces thro' the window of his cot,
And quits his easy bed; then o'er the field,   40
With lengthened swinging strides, betakes his way,
Bearing his spade and hoe across his shoulder,
Seen from afar clear glancing in the sun,
And with good will begins his daily work.
The sturdy sunburnt boy drives forth the cattle,
And vain of power, bawls to the lagging kine,
Who fain would stay to crop the tender shoots
Of the green tempting hedges as they pass;
Or beats the glistening bushes with his club,
To please his fancy with a shower of dew,   50
And frighten the poor birds who lurk within.
At every open door, thro' all the village,
Half-naked children, half-awake, are seen

Scratching their heads, and blinking to the light;
Till roused by degrees, they run about,
Or rolling in the sun, amongst the sand
Build many a little house, with heedful art.
The housewife tends within, her morning care;
And stooping 'midst her tubs of curdled milk,
With busy patience, draws the clear green whey   60
From the pressed sides of the pure snowy curd;
Whilst her brown dimpled maid, with tucked-up sleeve,
And swelling arm, assists her in her toil.
Pots smoke, pails rattle, and the warm confusion
Still thickens on them, till within its mould,
With careful hands, they press the well-wrought curd.

      So goes the morning, till the powerful sun
High in the heavens sends forth his strengthened beams,
And all the freshness of the morn is fled.
The sweating traveller throws his burden down,   70
And leans his weary shoulder 'gainst a tree.
The idle horse upon the grassy field
Rolls on his back, nor heeds the tempting clover.
The swain leaves off his labour, and returns
Slow to his house with heavy sober steps,
Where on the board his ready breakfast placed,
Invites the eye, and his right cheerful wife
Doth kindly serve him with unfeigned good will.
No sparkling dewdrops hang upon the grass;
Forth steps the mower with his glittering scythe,   80
In snowy shirt, and doublet all unbraced,
White moves he o'er the ridge, with sideling bend,
And lays the waving grass in many a heap.
In every field, in every swampy mead,
The cheerful voice of industry is heard;
The haycock rises, and the frequent rake
Sweeps on the yellow hay, in heavy wreaths,
Leaving the smooth green meadow bare behind.
The old and young, the weak and strong are there,
And, as they can, help on the cheerful work.   90
The father jeers his awkward half-grown lad,
Who trails his tawdry armful o'er the field,
Nor does he fear the jeering to repay.

The village oracle, and simple maid,
Jest in their turns, and raise the ready laugh;
For there authority, hard favoured, frowns not;
All are companions in the general glee,
And cheerful complaisance still thro' their roughness,
With placid look enlightens every face.
Some more advanced raise the towering rick,   100
Whilst on its top doth stand the parish toast
In loose attire, and swelling ruddy cheek;
With taunts and harmless mockery she receives
The tossed-up heaps from the brown gaping youth,
Who staring at her, takes his aim awry,
Whilst half the load comes tumbling on himself.
Loud is her laugh, her voice is heard afar;
Each mower, busied in the distant field,
The carter, trudging on his distant way,
The shrill sound know, cast up their hats in air,   110
And roar across the fields to catch her notice:
She waves her arm, and shakes her head at them,
And then renews her work with double spirit.
Thus do they jest, and laugh away their toil,
Till the bright sun, full in his middle course,
Shoots down his fiercest beams, which none may brave.
The stoutest arm hangs listless by its side,
And the broad-shouldered youth begins to fail.
But to the weary, lo! there comes relief!
A troop of welcome children, o'er the lawn,   120
With slow and wary steps, their burthens bring.
Some bear upon their heads large baskets, heaped
With piles of barley bread, and gusty cheese,
And some full pots of milk and cooling whey.
Beneath the branches of a spreading tree,
Or by the shadowy side of the tall rick,
They spread their homely fare, and seated round,
Taste all the pleasure that a feast can give.

       A drowsy indolence now hangs on all,
And every creature seeks some place of rest,   130
Screened from the violence of the oppressive heat,
No scattered flocks are seen upon the lawn,
Nor chirping birds among the bushes heard.

Within the narrow shadow of the cot
The sleepy dog lies stretched on his side,
Nor heeds the heavy-footed passenger;
At noise of feet but half his eyelid lifts,
Then gives a feeble growl, and sleeps again:
Whilst puss, less nice, e'en in the scorching window,
On t'other side, sits winking to the sun.   140
No sound is heard but humming of the bee,
For she alone retires not from her labour,
Nor leaves a meadow flower unsought for gain.

      Heavy and slow so pass the midday hours,
Till gently bending on the ridge's top,
The heavy-seeded grass begins to wave,
And the high branches of the slender poplar
Shiver aloft in air their rustling leaves.
Cool breathes the rising breeze, and with it wakes
The worn-out spirit from its state of stupor.   150
The lazy boy springs from his mossy bed,
To chase the gaudy tempting butterfly,
Who spreading on the grass its mealy wings,
Oft lights within his reach, e'en at his feet,
Yet still eludes his grasp, and o'er his head
Light hovering round, or mounted high in air
Tempts his young eye, and wearies out his limbs.
The drowsy dog, who feels the kindly breeze,
That passing o'er him, lifts his shaggy ear,
Begins to stretch him, on his legs half-raised,   160
Till fully waked, with bristling cocked-up tail,
He makes the village echo to his bark.

      But let us not forget the busy maid
Who, by the side of the clear pebbly stream,
Spreads out her snowy linens to the sun,
And sheds with liberal hand the crystal shower
O'er many a favourite piece of fair attire,
Revolving in her mind her gay appearance
In all this dress, at some approaching fair.
The dimpling half-checked smile, and muttering lip   170
Betray the secret workings of her fancy,
And flattering thoughts of the complacent mind.

There little vagrant bands of truant boys
Amongst the bushes try their harmless tricks;
Whilst some a-sporting in the shallow stream
Toss up the lashing water round their heads,
Or strive with wily art to catch the trout,
Or 'twixt their fingers grasp the slippery eel,
The shepherd-boy sits singing on the bank,
To pass away the weary lonely hours,   180
Weaving with art his little crown of rushes,
A guiltless easy crown that brings no care,
Which having made he places on his head,
And leaps and skips about, and bawls full loud
To some companion, lonely as himself,
Far in the distant field; or else delighted
To hear the echoed sound of his own voice
Returning answer from the neighbouring rock,
Holds no unpleasing converse with himself.

    Now weary labourers perceive, well-pleased,   190
The shadows lengthen, and the oppressive day
With all its toil fast wearing to an end.
The sun, far in the west, with sidelong beam
Plays on the yellow head of the round haycock,
And fields are checkered with fantastic shapes
Or tree, or shrub, or gate, or rugged stone,
All lengthened out, in antic disproportion,
Upon the darkened grass. –
They finish out their long and toilsome task.
Then, gathering up their rakes and scattered coats,   200
With the less cumbrous fragments of their feast,
Return right gladly to their peaceful homes.

    The village, lone and silent thro' the day,
Receiving from the fields its merry bands,
Sends forth its evening sound, confused but cheerful;
Whilst dogs and children, eager housewives' tongues,
And true-love ditties, in no plaintive strain,
By shrill-voiced maid, at open window sung;
The lowing of the home-returning kine,
The herd's low droning trump, and tinkling bell   210
Tied to the collar of his favourite sheep,

Makes no contemptible variety
To ears not over nice. –
With careless lounging gait, the sauntering youth
Upon his sweetheart's open window leans,
And as she turns about her buzzing wheel,
Diverts her with his jokes and harmless taunts.
Close by the cottage door, with placid mien,
The old man sits upon his seat of turf,
His staff with crooked head laid by his side,   220
Which oft the younger race in wanton sport,
Gambolling round him, slyly steal away,
And straddling o'er it, show their horsemanship
By raising round the clouds of summer sand,
While still he smiles, yet chides them for the trick,
His silver locks upon his shoulder spread,
And not ungraceful in his stoop of age.
No stranger passes him without regard;
And every neighbour stops to wish him well,
And ask him his opinion of the weather.   230
They fret not at the length of his discourse,
But listen with respect to his remarks
Upon the various seasons he remembers;
For well he knows the many diverse signs
Which do foretell high winds, or rain, or drought,
Or ought that may affect the rising crop.
The silken clad, who courtly breeding boast,
Their own discourse still sweetest to their ears,
May grumble at the old man's lengthened story,
But here it is not so. –   240

    From every chimney mounts the curling smoke,
Muddy and gray, of the new evening fire;
On every window smokes the family supper,
Set out to cool by the attentive housewife,
While cheerful groups at every door convened
Bawl across the narrow lane the parish news,
And oft the bursting laugh disturbs the air.
But see who comes to set them all agog!
The weary-footed pedlar with his pack.
How stiff he bends beneath his bulky load!   250
Covered with dust, slip-shod, and out at elbows;

His greasy hat sits backward on his head;
His thin straight hair divided on his brow
Hangs lank on either side his glistening cheeks,
And woebegone, yet vacant is his face.
His box he opens and displays his ware.
Full many a varied row of precious stones
Call forth their dazzling lustre to the light.
To the desiring maiden's wishful eye
The ruby necklace shows its tempting blaze: 260
The china buttons, stamped with love device,
Attract the notice of the gaping youth;
Whilst streaming garters, fastened to a pole,
Aloft in air their gaudy stripes display,
And from afar the distant stragglers lure.
The children leave their play and round him flock;
E'en sober aged grand-dame quits her seat,
Where by the door she twines her lengthened threads,
Her spindle stops, and lays her distaff by,
Then joins with step sedate the curious throng.   270
She praises much the fashions of her youth,
And scorns each gaudy nonsense of the day;
Yet not ill-pleased the glossy ribband views,
Uprolled, and changing hues with every fold,
New measured out to deck her daughter's head.

    Now red, but languid, the last weakly beams
Of the departing sun, across the lawn
Deep gild the top of the long sweepy ridge,
And shed a scattered brightness, bright but cheerless,
Between the openings of the rifted hills;   280
Which like the farewell looks of some dear friend,
That speaks him kind, yet sadden as they smile,
But only serve to deepen the low vale,
And make the shadows of the night more gloomy.
The varied noises of the cheerful village
By slow degrees now faintly die away,
And more distinct each feeble sound is heard
That gently steals adown the river's bed,
Or thro' the wood comes with the ruffling breeze.
The white mist rises from the swampy glens,   290
And from the dappled skirting of the heavens

Looks out the evening star. –
The lover skulking in the neighbouring copse,
(Whose half-seen form shown thro' the thickened air,
Large and majestic, makes the traveller start,
And spreads the story of the haunted grove,)
Curses the owl, whose loud ill-omened scream,
With ceaseless spite, robs from his watchful ear
The well-known footsteps of his darling maid;
And fretful, chases from his face the night-fly,   300
Who buzzing round his head doth often skim,
With fluttering wing, across his glowing cheek:
For all but him in deep and balmy sleep
Forget the toils of the oppressive day;
Shut is the door of every scattered cot,
And silence dwells within.

A REVERIE

Beside a spreading elm, from whose high boughs
Like knotted tufts the crow's light dwelling shows,
Where screened from northern blasts, and winter proof,
Snug stands the parson's barn with thatched roof;
At chaff-strewed door, where, in the morning ray,
The gilded motes in mazy circles play,
And sleepy Comrade in the sun is laid,
More grateful to the cur than neighbouring shade;
In snowy shirt unbraced, brown Robin stood,
And leant upon his flail in thoughtful mood: 10
His full round cheek where deeper flushes glow,
The dewy drops which glisten on his brow;
His dark cropped pate that erst at church or fair,
So smooth and silky, showed his morning's care,
Which all uncouth in matted locks combined,
Now, ends erect, defies the ruffling wind;
His neck-band loose, and hosen rumpled low,
A careful lad, nor slack at labour show.
Nor scraping chickens chirping 'mongst the straw,

Nor croaking rook o'erhead, nor chattering daw;   20
Loud-breathing cow amongst the rampy weeds,
Nor grunting sow that in the furrow feeds;
Nor sudden breeze that shakes the quaking leaves,
And lightly rustles thro' the scattered sheaves;
Nor floating straw that skims athwart his nose,
The deeply musing youth may discompose.
For Nelly fair, and blithest village maid,
Whose tuneful voice beneath the hedge-row shade,
At early milking, o'er the meadows born,
E'er cheered the ploughman's toil at rising morn: 30
The neatest maid that e'er, in linen gown,
Bore cream and butter to the market town:
The tightest lass, that with untutored air
E'er footed ale-house floor at wake or fair,
Since Easter last had Robin's heart possessed,
And many a time disturbed his nightly rest.
Full oft returning from the loosened plough,
He slacked his pace, and knit his thoughtful brow;
And oft ere half his thresher's task was o'er,
Would muse, with arms across, at cooling door: 40
His mind thus bent, with downcast eyes he stood,
And leant upon his flail in thoughtful mood.
His soul o'er many a soft remembrance ran,
And, muttering to himself, the youth began.

'Ah! happy is the man whose early lot
Hath made him master of a furnished cot;
Who trains the vine that round his window grows,
And after setting sun his garden hoes;
Whose wattled pales his own enclosure shield,
Who toils not daily in another's field.   50
Where'er he goes, to church or market town,
With more respect he and his dog are known:
A brisker face he wears at wake or fair
Nor views with longing eyes the pedlar's ware,
But buys at will or ribbands, gloves or beads,
And willing maidens to the ale-house leads:
And, oh! secure from toils which cumber life,
He makes the maid he loves an easy wife.
Ah, Nelly! canst thou with contented mind,

Become the helpmate of a labouring hind,   60
And share his lot, whate'er the chances be,
Who hath no dower, but love, to fix on thee?
Yes, gayest maid may meekest matron prove,
And things of little note may 'token love.
When from the church thou camest at eventide
And I and red-haired Susan by thy side,
I pulled the blossoms from the bending tree,
And some to Susan gave, and some to thee;
Thine were the best, and well thy smiling eye
The difference marked, and guessed the reason why.   70
When on a holyday we rambling strayed,
And passed old Hodge's cottage in the glade;
Neat was the garden dressed, sweet hummed the bee,
I wished both cot and Nelly made for me;
And well methought thy very eyes revealed
The selfsame wish within thy breast concealed.
When artful, once, I sought my love to tell,
And spoke to thee of one who loved thee well,
You saw the cheat, and jeering homeward hied,
Yet secret pleasure in thy looks I spied.   80
Ay, gayest maid may meekest matron prove,
And smaller signs than these have tokened love.'

      Now, at a distance, on the neighbouring plain,
With creaking wheels slow comes the heavy wain:
High on its towering load a maid appears,
And Nelly's voice sounds shrill in Robin's ears.
Quick from his hand he throws the cumbrous flail,
And leaps with lightsome limbs the enclosing pale.
O'er field and fence he scours, and furrow wide,
With wakened Comrade barking by his side;   90
Whilst tracks of trodden grain, and sidelong hay,
And broken hedge-flowers sweet, mark his impetuous way.

A DISAPPOINTMENT

On village green, whose smooth and well-worn sod,
Cross-pathed with every gossip's foot is trod;
By cottage door where playful children run,
And cats and curs sit basking in the sun:
Where o'er the earthen seat the thorn is bent,
Cross-armed, and back to wall, poor William leant.
His bonnet broad drawn o'er his gathered brow,
His hanging lip and lengthened visage show
A mind but ill at ease. With motions strange,
His listless limbs their wayward postures change;   10
Whilst many a crooked line and curious maze,
With clouted shoon, he on the sand portrays.
The half-chewed straw fell slowly from his mouth,
And to himself low muttering spoke the youth.
        'How simple is the lad! And reft of skill,
Who thinks with love to fix a woman's will:
Who every Sunday morn, to please her sight,
Knots up his neck-cloth gay, and hosen white:
Who for her pleasure keeps his pockets bare,
And half his wages spends on pedlar's ware;   20
When every niggard clown, or dotard old,
Who hides in secret nooks his oft told gold,
Whose field or orchard tempts with all her pride,
At little cost may win her for his bride;
Whilst all the meed her silly lover gains
Is but the neighbours' jeering for his pains.
On Sunday last when Susan's banns were read,
And I astonished sat with hanging head,
Cold grew my shrinking limbs, and loose my knee,
Whilst every neighbour's eye was fixed on me.   30
Ah, Sue! when last we worked at Hodge's hay,
And still at me you jeered in wanton play;
When last at fair, well pleased by show-man's stand,
You took the new-bought fairing from my hand;
When at old Hobb's you sung that song so gay,
Sweet William still the burthen of the lay,
I little thought, alas! the lots were cast,
That thou shouldst be another's bride at last:
And had, when last we tripped it on the green

And laughed at stiff-backed Rob, small thought I ween,   40
Ere yet another scanty month was flown,
To see thee wedded to the hateful clown.
Ay, lucky swain, more gold thy pockets line;
But did these shapely limbs resemble thine,
I'd stay at home, and tend the household gear,
Nor on the green with other lads appear.
Ay, lucky swain, no store thy cottage lacks,
And round thy barn thick stand the sheltered stacks;
But did such features hard my visage grace,
I'd never budge the bonnet from my face.   50
Yet let it be: it shall not break my ease:
He best deserves who doth the maiden please.
Such silly cause no more shall give me pain,
Nor ever maiden cross my rest again.
Such grizzly suitors with their taste agree,
And the black fiend may take them all for me!'

      Now thro' the village rise confused sounds,
Hoarse lads, and children shrill, and yelping hounds.
Straight every matron at the door is seen,
And pausing hedgers on their mattocks lean.   60
At every narrow lane, and alley mouth,
Loud laughing lasses stand, and joking youth.
A bridal band tricked out in colours gay,
With minstrels blithe before to cheer the way,
From clouds of curling dust which onward fly,
In rural splendour break upon the eye.
As in their way they hold so gaily on,
Caps, beads, and buttons glancing in the sun,
Each village wag, with eye of roguish cast,
Some maiden jogs, and vents the ready jest;   70
Whilst village toasts the passing belles deride,
And sober matrons marvel at their pride.
But William, head erect, with settled brow,
In sullen silence viewed the passing show;
And oft he scratched his pate with manful grace,
And scorned to pull the bonnet o'er his face;
But did with steady look unmoved wait,
Till hindmost man had turned the churchyard gate;
Then turned him to his cot with visage flat,

Where honest Tray upon the threshold sat.   80
Up jumped the kindly beast his hand to lick,
And, for his pains, received an angry kick.
Loud shuts the flapping door with thundering din;
The echoes round their circling course begin,
From cot to cot, in wide progressive swell,
Deep groans the churchyard wall and neighbouring dell,
And Tray, responsive, joins with long and piteous yell.

A LAMENTATION

Where ancient broken wall encloses round,
From tread of lawless feet, the hallowed ground,
And sombre yews their dewy branches wave
O'er many a motey stone and mounded grave:
Where parish church, confusedly to the sight,
With deeper darkness prints the shades of night,
And mouldering tombs uncouthly gape around,
And rails and fallen stones bestrew the ground;
In loosened garb deranged, with scattered hair,
His bosom open to the nightly air,   10
Lone, o'er a new heaped grave poor Basil bent,
And to himself began his simple plaint.

          'Alas! How cold thy home! How low thou art!
Who wert the pride and mistress of my heart.
The fallen leaves light rustling o'er thee pass,
And o'er thee waves the rank and dewy grass.
The new-laid sods in decent order tell
How narrow now the space where thou must dwell.
Now rough and wintry winds may on thee beat,
And drizzly drifting snow, and summer's heat;   20
Each passing season rub, for woe is me!
Or storm, or sunshine, is the same to thee.
Ah, Mary! lovely was thy slender form,
And sweet thy cheerful brow, that knew no storm.

3 *Bothwell Church, Lanarkshire* by H. Maliphant (early nineteenth-century)

represents the church in which Joanna Baillie was baptised and of which her father was minister until she was seven. Joanna Baillie might have been drawing on her memories of Bothwell Church graveyard in writing 'A Lamentation'

Thy steps were graceful on the village green,
As tho' thou hadst some courtly lady been:
At church or market, still the gayest lass,
Each youngster slacked his speed to see thee pass.
At early milking, tuneful was thy lay,
And sweet thy homeward song at close of day;   30
But sweeter far, and every youth's desire,
Thy cheerful converse by the evening fire.
Alas! No more thou'lt foot the grassy sward!
No song of thine shall ever more be heard!
Yet now they trip it lightly on the green,
As blithe and gay as thou hadst never been:
The careless youngster whistles lightsome by,
And other maidens catch his roving eye:
Around the evening fire, with little care,
The neighbours sit, and scarcely miss thee there;   40
And when the night advancing darkens round,
They to their rest retire, and slumber sound.
But Basil cannot rest; his days are sad,
And long his nights upon the weary bed.
Yet still in broken dreams thy form appears,
And still my bosom proves a lover's fears.
I guide thy footsteps through the tangled wood;
I catch thee sinking in the boisterous flood;
I shield thy bosom from the threatened stroke;
I clasp thee falling from the headlong rock;   50
But ere we reach the dark and dreadful deep,
High heaves my troubled breast, I wake, and weep.
At every wailing of the midnight wind
Thy lowly dwelling comes into my mind.
When rain beats on my roof, wild storms abroad,
I think upon thy bare and beaten sod;
I hate the comfort of a sheltered home,
And hie me forth o'er fenceless fields to roam:
I leave the paths of men for dreary waste,
And bare my forehead to the howling blast.   60
O Mary! loss of thee hath fixed my doom:
This world around me is a weary gloom:
Dull heavy musings down my spirits weigh,
I cannot sleep by night, nor work by day.
Or wealth or pleasure slowest minds inspire,

But cheerless is their toil who nought desire.
Let happier friends divide my farmers' flock;
Cut down my grain, and sheer my little flock;
For now my only care on earth shall be
Here every Sunday morn to visit thee;   70
And in the holy church, with heart sincere,
And humble mind, our worthy curate hear:
He best can tell, when earthly cares are past,
The surest way to meet with thee at last.
I'll thus a while a weary life abide,
Till wasting Time hath laid me by thy side;
For now on earth there is no place for me,
Nor peace, nor slumber, till I rest with thee.'

    Loud, from the lofty spire, with piercing knell,
Solemn, and awful, tolled the parish bell;   80
A later hour than rustics deem it meet
That churchyard ground be trod by mortal feet,
The wailing lover startled at the sound,
And raised his head and cast his eyes around.
The gloomy pile in strengthened horror lowered,
Large and majestic every object towered:
Dim thro' the gloom they showed their forms unknown,
And tall and ghastly rose each whitened stone:
Aloft the waking screech owl 'gan to sing,
And past him skimmed the bat with flapping wing,   90
The fears of nature woke within his breast;
He left the hallowed spot of Mary's rest,
And sped his way the churchyard wall to gain,
Then checked his coward heart, and turned again.
The shadows round a deeper horror wear;
A deeper silence hangs upon his ear;
A stiller rest is o'er the settled scene;
His fluttering heart recoils, and shrinks again.
With hasty steps he measures back the ground,
And leaps with summoned force the churchyard bound;   100
Then home with knocking limbs, and quickened breath,
His footstep urges from the place of death.

AN ADDRESS TO THE MUSES

Ye tuneful sisters of the lyre,
Who dreams and fantasies inspire;
Who over poesy preside,
And on a lofty hill abide
Above the ken of mortal fight,
Fain would I sing of you, could I address ye right.

Thus known, your power of old was sung,
And temples with your praises rung;
And when the song of battle rose,
Or kindling wine, or lovers' woes,   10
The poet's spirit inly burned,
And still to you his upcast eyes were turned.

The youth all wrapped in vision bright,
Beheld your robes of flowing white:
And knew your forms benignly grand,
An awful, but a lovely band;
And felt your inspiration strong,
And warmly poured his rapid lay along.

The aged bard all heavenward glowed,
And hailed you daughters of a god: 20
Tho' to his dimmer eyes were seen
Nor graceful form, nor heavenly mien,
Full well he felt that ye were near,
And heard you in the blast that shook his hoary hair.

Ye lightened up the valley's bloom,
And deeper spread the forest's gloom;
And lofty hill sublimer stood,
And grander rose the mighty flood;
For then Religion lent her aid,
And o'er the mind of man your sacred empire spread.   30

Tho' rolling ages now are past,
And altars low, and temples waste;
Tho' rites and oracles are o'er,
And gods and heroes rule no more;

Your fading honours still remain,
And still your votaries call, a long and motley train.

They seek you not on hill and plain,
Nor court you in the sacred fane;
Nor meet you in the midday dream,
Upon the bank of hallowed stream;   40
Yet still for inspiration sue,
And still each lifts his fervent prayer to you.

He knows ye not in woodland gloom,
But woos ye in the shelfed room;
And seeks you in the dusty nook,
And meets you in the lettered book;
Full well he knows you by your names,
And still with poets faith your presence claims.

The youthful poet, pen in hand,
All by the side of blotted stand,   50
In reverie deep, which none may break,
Sits rubbing of his beardless cheek;
And well his inspiration knows,
E'en by the dewy drops that trickle o'er his nose.

The tuneful sage of riper fame,
Perceives you not in heated frame;
But at the conclusion of his verse,
Which still his muttering lips rehearse,
Oft waves his hand in grateful pride,
And owns the heavenly power that did his fancy guide.   60

O lovely sisters! is it true,
That they are all inspired by you?
And while they write, with magic charmed,
And high enthusiasm warmed,
We may not question heavenly lays,
For well I wot, they give you all the praise.

O lovely sisters! well it shows
How wide and far your bounty flows:
They why from me withhold your beams?

Unvisited of heavenly dreams,   70
Whene'er I aim at heights sublime,
Still downward am I called to seek some stubborn rhyme.

No hasty lightning breaks the gloom,
Nor flashing thoughts unsought for come,
Nor fancies wake in time of need;
I labour much with little speed;
And when my studied task is done,
Too well, alas! I mark it for my own.

Yet should you never smile on me,
And rugged still my verses be;   80
Unpleasing to the tuneful train,
Who only prize a flowing strain;
And still the learned scorn my lays,
I'll lift my heart to you, and sing your praise.

Your varied ministry to trace,
Your honoured names and godlike race,
And lofty bowers where fountains flow,
They'll better sing who better know;
I praise ye not with Grecian lyre,
Nor will I hail ye daughters of a heathen fire.   90

Ye are the spirits who preside
In earth, and air, and ocean wide;
In hissing flood, and crackling fire;
In horror dread, and tumult dire;
In stilly calm, and stormy wind,
And rule the answering changes in the human mind.

High on the tempest-beaten hill,
Your misty shapes ye shift at will;
The wild fantastic clouds ye form;
Your voice is in the midnight storm,   100
Whilst in the dark and lonely hour,
Oft starts the boldest heart, and owns your secret power.

From you, when growling storms are past,
And lightning ceases on the waste,

And when the scene of blood is o'er,
And groans of death are heard no more,
Still holds the mind each parted form,
Like after echoing of the o'er passed storm.

When closing glooms o'erspread the day,
And what we love has passed away,   110
Ye kindly bid each pleasing scene
Within the bosom still remain,
Like moons who doth their watches run
With the reflected brightness of the parted sun.

The shining day, and nightly shade,
The cheerful plain and gloomy glade,
The homeward flocks, and shepherds play,
The busy hamlet's closing day,
Full many a breast with pleasures swell,
Who ne'er shall have the gift of words to tell.   120

Oft when the moon looks from on high,
And black around the shadows lie;
And bright the sparkling waters gleam,
And rushes rustle by the stream,
Shrill sounds, and fairy forms are known
By simple 'nighted swains, who wander late alone.

Ye kindle up the inward glow,
Ye strengthen every outward show;
Ye overleap the strongest bar,
And join what Nature sunders far: 130
And visit oft in fancies wild,
The breast of learned sage, and simple child.

From him who wears a monarch's crown,
To the unlettered artless clown,
All in some strange and lonely hour
Have felt, unsought, your secret power,
And loved your roving fancies well,
You add but to the bard the art to tell.

Ye mighty spirits of the song,
To whom the poets' prayers belong,   140
My lowly bosom to inspire,
And kindle with your sacred fire,
Your wild obscuring heights to brave,
Is boon, alas! too great for me to crave.

But O, such sense of matter bring!
As they who feel and never sing
Wear on their hearts, it will avail
With simple words to tell my tale;
And still contented will I be,
Tho' greater inspirations never fall to me.   150

THE STORM-BEAT MAID
(SOMEWHAT AFTER THE STYLE
OF OUR OLD ENGLISH BALLADS)

All shrouded in the winter snow,
        The maiden held her way;
Nor chilly winds that roughly blow,
        Nor dark night could her stay.

O'er hill and dale, through bush and briar,
        She on her journey kept;
Save often when she 'gan to tire,
        She stopped awhile and wept.

Wild creatures left their caverns drear,
        To raise their nightly yell;   10
But little doth the bosom fear,
        Where inward troubles dwell.

No watch-light from the distant spire,
        To cheer the doom so deep,
Nor twinkling star, nor cottage fire
        Did thro' the darkness peep.

4 *Bothwell Castle* by Paul Sandby (1725–1809)

is a representation of an historic landmark in Lanarkshire where Baillie grew up.
She was familiar with the history of this castle, and might have been drawing on her
memories of these castle ruins in her mock-medieval ballad, 'A Storm-Beat Maid'

Yet heedless still she held her way,
    Nor feared the crag nor dell;
Like ghost that thro' the gloom to stray,
    Wakes with the midnight bell.   20

Now night thro' her dark watches ran,
    Which lock the peaceful mind;
And thro' the neighbouring hamlets 'gan
    To wake the yawning hind.

Yet bark of dog, nor village cock,
    That spoke the morning near;
Nor gray light trembling on the rock,
    Her 'nighted mind could cheer.

The whirling flail, and clacking mill
    Wake with the early day;   30
And careless children, loud and shrill,
    With newmade snowballs play.

And as she passed each cottage door,
    They did their gambols cease;
And old men shook their locks so hoar,
    And wished her spirit peace.

For sometimes slow, and sometimes fast,
    She held her wavering pace;
Like early spring's inconstant blast,
    That ruffles evening's face.   40

At length with weary feet she came,
    Where in a sheltering wood,
Whose master bore no humble name,
    A stately castle stood.

The open gate, and smoking fires,
    Which cloud the air so thin;
And shrill bell tinkling from the spires,
    Bespoke a feast within.

With busy looks, and hasty tread,
    The servants cross the hall;   50
And many a page, in buskins red,
    Await the master's call.

Fair streaming bows of bridal white
    On every shoulder played;
And clean, in lily kerchief dight,
    Tripped every household maid.

She asked for neither lord nor dame,
    Nor who the mansion owned;
But straight into the hall she came,
    And sat her on the ground.   60

The busy crew all crowded nigh,
    And round the stranger stared;
But still she rolled her wandering eye,
    Nor for their questions cared.

'What dost thou want, thou storm-beat maid,
    That thou these portals passed?
Ill suiteth here thy looks dismayed,
    Thou are no bidden guest.'

'O chide not!' said a gentle page,
    And wiped his tear-wet cheek,   70
'Who would not shun the winter's rage?
    The wind is cold and bleak.

Her robe is stiff with drizzly snow,
    And rent her mantle grey;
None ever bade the wretched go
    Upon his wedding-day.'

Then to his lord he hied him straight,
    Where round on silken seat
Sat many a courteous dame and knight,
    And made obeisance meet.   80

'There is a stranger in your hall,
          Who wears no common mien;
Hard were the heart, as flinty wall,
          That would not take her in.

A fairer dame in hall or bower
          Mine eyes did ne'er behold;
Tho' sheltered in no father's tower,
          And turned out to the cold.

Her face is like an early morn,
          Dimmed with the nightly dew;   90
Her skin is like the sheeted torn,
          Her eyes are watery blue.

And tall and slender is her form,
          Like willow o'er the brook;
But on her brow there broods a storm,
          And restless is her look.

And well her troubled motions show
          The tempest in her mind;
Like the unsheltered sapling bough
          Vexed with the wintry wind.   100

Her head droops on her ungirt breast,
          And scattered is her hair;
Yet lady braced in courtly vest
          Was never half so fair.'

Reverse, and cold the turning blood
          The bridegroom's cheek forsook:
He shook and staggered as he stood,
          And faltered as he spoke.

'So soft and fair I know a maid,
          There is but only she;   110
A wretched man her love betrayed,
          And wretched let him be.'

Deep frowning, turned the bride's dark eye,
    For bridal morn unmeet;
With trembling steps her lord did hie
    The stranger fair to greet.

Tho' loose in scattered weeds arrayed,
    And ruffled with the storm;
Like lambkin from its fellows strayed,
    He knew her graceful form.   120

But when he spied her sunken eye,
    And features sharp and wan,
He heaved a deep and heavy sigh,
    And down the big tears ran.

'Why droops thy head, thou lovely maid,
    Upon thy hand of snow?
Is it because thy love betrayed,
    That thou art brought so low?'

Quick from her eye the keen glance came
    Who questioned her to see: 130
And oft she muttered o'er his name,
    And wist not it was he.

Full hard against his writhing brows
    His clenched hands he pressed;
Full high his labouring bosom rose,
    And rent its silken vest.

'O cursed be the golden price,
    That did my baseness prove!
And cursed be my friends' advice,
    That willed me from thy love!   140

And cursed be the woman's art,
    That lured me to her snare!
And cursed be the faithless heart
    That left thee to despair!

Yet now I'll hold thee to my side,
    Tho' worthless I have been,
Nor fiends, nor wealth, nor dizened bride,
    Shall ever stand between.

When thou art weary and depressed,
    I'll lull thee to thy sleep;   150
And when dark fancies vex thy breast,
    I'll sit by thee and weep.

I'll tend thee like a restless child
    Where'er thy rovings be;
Nor gesture keen, nor eyeball wild,
    Shall turn my love from thee.

Night shall not hang cold o'er thy head,
    And I securely lie;
Nor drizzly clouds upon thee shed,
    And I in covert dry.   160

I'll share the cold blast on the heath,
    I'll share thy wants and pain:
Nor friend nor foe, nor life nor death,
    Shall ever make us twain.'

AN ADDRESS TO THE NIGHT:
A FEARFUL MIND

Uncertain, awful as the gloom of death,
The Night's grim shadows cover all beneath.
Shapeless and black is every object round,
And lost in thicker gloom the distant bound.
Each swelling height is clad with dimmer shades,
And deeper darkness marks the hollow glades.
The moon in heavy clouds her glory veils,
And slow along their passing darkness sails;
While lesser clouds in parted fragments roam,
And red stars glimmer thro' the river's gloom.   10

Nor cheerful voice is heard from man's abode,
Nor sounding footsteps on the neighbouring road;
Nor glimmering fire the distant cottage tells;
On all around a fearful stillness dwells:
The mingled noise of industry is laid,
And silence deepens with the nightly shade.
Though still the haunts of men, and shut their light,
Thou art not silent, dark mysterious Night.
The cries of savage creatures wildly break
Upon thy quiet; birds ill-omened shriek: 20
Commotions strange disturb the rustling trees;
And heavy plaints come on the passing breeze.
Far on the lonely waste, and distant way,
Unwonted sounds are heard, unknown of day.
With shrilly screams the haunted cavern rings;
And heavy treading of unearthly things
Sounds loud and hollow thro' the ruined dome;
Yes, voices issue from the secret tomb.

But lo! a sudden flow of bursting light!
What wild surrounding scenes break on the sight!   30
Huge rugged rocks uncouthly lower on high,
Whilst on the plain their lengthened shadows lie.
The wooded banks in streamy brightness glow;
And waving darkness skirts the flood below.
The roving shadow hastens o'er the stream;
And like a ghost's pale shroud the waters gleam.
Black fleeting shapes across the valley stray:
Gigantic forms tower on the distant way:
The sudden winds in wheeling eddies change:
'Tis all confused, unnatural, and strange.   40
Now all again in horrid gloom is lost:
Wild wakes the breeze like sound of distant host:
Bright shoots along the swift returning light:
Succeeding shadows close the startled sight.
Some restless spirit holds the nightly sway:
Long is the wild, and doubtful is my way.
Inconstant Night, whate'er thy changes be,
It suits not man to be alone with thee.
Lo! for the sheltering roof of lowest hind,
Secure to rest with others of my kind!   50

AN ADDRESS TO THE NIGHT:
A DISCONTENTED MIND

How thick the clouds of night are ranged o'er head!
Confounding darkness o'er the earth is spread.
The clouded moon her cheering countenance hides;
And feeble stars, between the ragged sides
Of broken clouds, with unavailing ray,
Look thro' to mock the traveller on his way.
Tree, bush, and rugged rock, and hollow dell,
In deeper shades their forms confusedly tell,
To cheat the weary wanderer's doubtful eye;
Whilst chilly passing winds come ruffling by;   10
And tangled briars perplex the darkened pass;
And slimy reptiles glimmer on the grass;
And stinging night-flies spend their curled spite;
Unhospitable are thy shades, O Night!

    Now hard suspicion bars the creaking door;
And safe within the selfish worldlings snore:
And wealthy fools are warm in downy bed:
And houseless beggars shelter in the shed:
And nestling coveys cower beneath the brake;
While prowling mischief only is awake.   20
Each hole and den sends forth its cursed brood,
And savage bloody creatures range the wood.
The thievish vagrant plies his thriftless trade
Beneath the friendly shelter of the shade;
Whilst boldest risk the lawless robber braves:
The day for fools was made, and night for knaves.

    O welcome, kindly moon! Thy light display,
And guide a weary traveller on his way.
Hill, wood, and valley, brighten in her beam;
And wavy silver glitters on the stream.   30
The distant pathway shows distinct and clear,
From far inviting, but perplexed when near.
For blackening shadows add deceitful length,
And lesser objects gain unwonted strength;
Each step misguiding; to the eye unknown,
The shining gutter, from the glistening stone;

While crossing shadows checker o'er the ground,
The more perplexing for the brightness round.
Deceitful are thy smiles, untoward Night!
Thy gloom is better than misguiding light.   40
Then welcome is yon cloud that onward sails,
And all this glary show in darkness veils.
But see how soon the fleeting shade is past,
And streamy brightness shoots across the waste.
Now fly the shadows borne upon the wind;
Succeeding brightness fast behind.
And now it lowers again. Inconstant Night,
Confound thy freaks! be either dark or light.
Yet let them come; whate'er thy changes be,
I was a fool to put my trust in thee.   50

AN ADDRESS TO THE NIGHT:
A SORROWFUL MIND

How lone and dreary hangs the sombre Night
O'er wood and valley, stream and craggy height!
While nearer objects, bush, and waving bough,
Their dark uncertain forms but dimly show;
Like those with which disturbed fancies teem,
And shape the scenery of a gloomy dream.
The moon is covered with her sable shroud;
And o'er the heavens rove many a dusky cloud;
Thro' ragged rents the paly sky is seen,
And feebly glance the twinkling stars between: 10
Whilst earth below is wrapt in stilly gloom,
All sad and silent as the closed tomb.

No bleating flock is heard upon the vale;
Nor lowing kine upon the open dale;
Nor voice of hunter on the lonely heath;
Nor sound of traveller on the distant path.
Shut is the fenced door of man's abode;
And ruffling breezes only are abroad.

How mournful is thy voice, O nightly gale!
Across the wood, or down the narrow vale;   20
And sad, tho' secret and unknown they be,
The sighs of woeful hearts that wake with thee.
For now no friends the haunts of sorrows seek;
Tears hang unchidden on the mourner's cheek:
No side-look vexes from the curious eye;
Nor calm reproving reasoner is by:
The kindly cumbrous visitor is gone,
And laden spirits love to sigh alone.
O Night! wild sings the wind, deep lowers the shade;
Thy robe is gloomy, and thy voice is sad: 30
But weary souls confined in earthly cell
Are deep in kindred gloom, and love thee well.

            But now the veiling darkness passes by;
The moon unclouded holds the middle sky.
A soft and mellow light is o'er the wood;
And silvery pureness sparkles on the flood.
White tower the cliffs from many a craggy breach;
The brown heath shows afar its dreary stretch.
While fairer as the brightened object swells,
Fast by its side the darker shadow dwells: 40
The lofty mountains form the deeper glade,
And keener light but marks the blacker shade.
Then welcome yonder clouds that swiftly sail,
And o'er yon glary opening draw the veil.
But ah! too swiftly flies the friendly shade!
Returning brightness travels up the glade,
And all is light again. O fickle Night!
No traveller is here to bless thy light.
I seek nor home, nor shed; I have no way:
Why send thy beams to one that cannot stray?   50
Or wood, or desert, is the same to me;
O lower again, and let me rest with thee!

AN ADDRESS TO THE NIGHT:
A JOYFUL MIND

The warping gloom of night is gathered round;
And varied darkness marks the uneven ground.
A dimmer shade is on the mountain's brow,
And deeper lowers the lengthened vale below;
While nearer objects all enlarged and dark,
Their strange and shapeless forms uncouthly mark;
Which thro' muddy night are dimly shown,
Like old companions in a garb unknown.
The heavy sheeted clouds are spread on high,
And streaky darkness bounds the farther sky: 10
And swift along the lighter vagrants sweep,
Whilst clear stars thro' their river edges peep.
Soft thro' each ragged breach, and streamy rent,
And open gaps in dusky circle pent,
The upper heaven looks serenely bright
In dappled gold, and snowy fleeces dight:
And on the middle current lightly glides
The lesser cloud, with silver wreathy sides.
In sudden gusts awakes the nightly breeze
Across the wood, and rustles thro' the trees;   20
Or whistles on the plain with eddying sweep;
Or issues from the glen in wailings deep,
Which die away upon the open vale:
Whilst in the pauses of the ruffling gale
The buzzing night-fly rises from the ground,
And wings his flight in many a mazy round;
And lonely owls begin their nightly strain,
So hateful to the ear of benighted swain.
Thou dost the weary traveller mislead;
Thy voice is roughsome, and uncouth thy weed,   30
O gloomy Night! for black thy shadows be,
And fools have raised a bad report on thee.
Yet art thou free and friendly to the gay,
And light hearts prize thee equal to the day.

        Now tiresome plodding folks are gone to rest;
And soothing slumber locks the careful breast.
And telltale friends, and wise advisers snore;

And softly slipshod youths unbar the door.
Now footsteps echo far, and watch-dogs bark;
Worms glow, and cats' eyes glitter in the dark.   40
The vagrant lover crosses moor and hill,
And near the lowly cottage whistles shrill:
Or, bolder grown, beneath the friendly shade,
Taps at the window of his favourite maid;
Who from above his simple tale receives,
Whilst stupid matrons start, and think of thieves.
Now daily fools unbar the narrow soul,
All wise and generous o'er the nightly bowl.
The haunted wood receives its motley host,
(By traveller shunned) tho' neither fag nor ghost;   50
And there the crackling bonfire blazes red,
While merry vagrants feast beneath the shed.
From sleepless beds unquiet spirits rise,
And cunning wags put on their borrowed guise:
Whilst silly maidens mutter o'er their boon,
And crop their fairy weeds beneath the moon:
And harmless plotters slyly take the road,
And trick and playful mischief is abroad.

        But, lo! the moon looks forth in splendour bright,
Fair and unclouded, from her middle height.   60
The puffing cloud unveils her kindly ray,
And slowly sails its weary length away:
While broken fragments from its fleecy side,
In dusky bands before it swiftly glide;
Their misty texture changing with the wind,
A strange and scattered group, of motley kind
As ever earth or fruitful ocean fed,
Or even youthful poets fancy bred.
His surgy length the wreathing serpent trails,
And by his side the rugged camel sails: 70
The winged griffith follows close behind,
And spreads his dusky pinions to the wind.
Athwart the sky in scattered bands they range
From shape to shape, transformed in endless change;
Then piecemeal torn, in ragged portions stray,
Or thinly spreading, slowly melt away.
A softer brightness covers all below;

Hill, dale, and wood, in mellow colour's glow.
High towers the whitened rock in added strength;
The brown heath shows afar its dreary length.   80
The winding river glitters on the vale;
And gilded trees wave in the passing gale.
Upon the ground each blackening shadow lies,
And hasty darkness o'er the valley flies.
Wide sheeting shadows travel o'er the plain,
And swiftly close upon the varied scene.
Return, O lovely moon! and look from high,
All stately riding in thy mottled sky.
Yet, O thy beams in hasty visits come!
As swiftly followed by the fleeting gloom.   90
O Night! thy smiles are short, and short thy shade;
Thou art a freakish friend, and all unstayed:
Yet from thy varied changes who are free?
Full many an honest friend resembles thee.
Then let my doubtful footsteps darkling stray,
Thy next fair beam will set me on my way:
E'en take thy freedom, whether rough or kind,
I came not forth to quarrel with the wind.

TO FEAR

O thou! before whose haggard eyes
A thousand images arise,
Whose forms of horror none may see,
But with a soul disturbed by thee!
Wilt thou forever haunt mankind,
And glare upon the darkened mind!
Whene'er thou enterest a breast,
Then robbed it of its joy and rest;
And terrible, and strange to tell,
On what that mind delights to dwell.   10
The ruffian's knife with reeking blade,
The stranger murdered in his bed:
The howling wind, the raging deep,
The sailor's cries, the sinking ship:

The awful thunder breaking round:
The yawning gulf, the rocking ground:
The precipice, whose lowering brow
O'erhangs the horrid deep below;
And tempts the wretch, worn out with strife,
Of worldly cares, to end his life.   20

          But when thou raisest to the sight
Unearthly forms that walk the night,
The chilly blood, with magic art,
Runs backward to the stoutest heart.
Lo! in his post the soldier stands!
The deadly weapon in his hands.
In front of death he rushes on,
Renown with life is cheaply won,
Whilst all his soul with ardour burns,
And to the thickest danger turns.   30
But see the man alone, unbent,
A churchyard near, and twilight spent,
Returning late to his abode,
Upon an unfrequented road:
No choice is left, his feet must tread
The awful dwelling of the dead.
In foul mist doth the pale moon wade,
No twinkling star breaks thro' the shade:
Thick rows of trees increase the gloom,
And awful silence of the tomb.   40
Swift to his thoughts, unbidden, throng
Full many a tale, forgotten long,
Of ghosts, who at the dead of night
Walk round their graves all wrapt in white,
And o'er the churchyard dark and drear,
Beckon the traveller to draw near:
And restless sprites, who from the ground,
Just as the midnight clock doth sound,
Rise slowly to a dreadful height,
Then vanish quickly from the sight: 50
And wretches who, returning home,
By chance have stumbled near some tomb,
Athwart a coffin or a bone,
And three times heard a hollow groan;

With fearful steps he takes his way,
And shrinks, and wishes it were day.
He starts and quakes at his own tread,
But dare not turn about his head.
Some sound he hears on every side;
And thro' the trees strange phantoms glide.   60
His heart beats thick against his breast,
And hardly stays within its chest:
Wild and unsettled are his eyes;
His quickened hairs begin to rise:
Ghastly and strong his features grow;
The cold dew trickles from his brow;
Whilst grinning beat his clattering teeth,
And loosened knock his joints beneath.
As to the charnel he draws nigh
The whitened tombstone strikes his eye: 70
He starts, he stops, his eyeballs glare,
And settle in a deathlike stare:
Deep hollow sounds ring in his ear;
Such sounds as dying wretches hear
When the grim dreaded tyrant calls,
A horrid sound, he groans and falls.

      Thou dost our fairest hope destroy;
Thou art a gloom o'er every joy;
Unheeded let my dwelling be,
O fear! But far removed from thee!   80

A MOTHER TO HER WAKING INFANT

Now in thy dazzling half-op'd eye,
Thy curled nose, and lip awry,
Thy uphoist arms, and noddling head,
And little chin with crystal spread,
Poor helpless thing! what do I see,
      That I should sing of thee?

From thy poor tongue no accents come,
Which can but rub thy toothless gum:
Small understanding boasts thy face,
Thy shapeless limbs nor step, nor grace: 10
A few short words thy feats may tell,
          And yet I love thee well.

When sudden wakes the bitter shriek,
And redder swells thy little cheek;
When rattled keys thy woe beguile,
And thro' the wet eye gleams the smile,
Still for thy weakly self is spent
          Thy little silly plaint.

But when thy friends are in distress,
Thou'lt laugh and chuckle ne'er the less;   20
Nor e'en with sympathy be smitten,
Tho' all are sad but thee and kitten;
Yet little varlet that thou art,
          Thou twitchest at the heart.

Thy rosy cheek so soft and warm;
Thy pinky hand, and dimpled arm;
Thy silken locks that scantly peep,
With gold-tipped ends, where circle deep,
Around thy neck in harmless grace,
So soft and sleekly hold their place,   30
Might harder hearts with kindness fill,
          And gain our right good will.

Each passing clown bestows his blessing,
Thy mouth is worn with old wives' kissing;
E'en lighter looks the gloomy eye
Of surly sense, when thou art by;
And yet, I think, whoe'er they be,
          They love thee not like me.

Perhaps when time shall add a few
Short months to thee, thou'lt love me too;   40
Then wilt thou through life's weary way,
Become my sure and cheering stay;

Wilt care for me, and be my hold,
    When I am weak and old.

Thou'lt listen to my lengthened tale,
And pity me when I am frail –
But see, the sweepy spinning fly
Upon the window takes thine eye.
Go to thy little senseless play;
    Thou dost not heed my lay.   50

A CHILD TO HIS SICK GRANDFATHER

Grand-dad, they say you're old and frail,
Your stocked legs begin to fail:
Your knobbed stick (that was my horse)
Can scarce support your bended corse,
While back to wall, you lean so sad,
    I'm vexed to see you, dad.

You used to smile and stroke my head,
And tell me how good children did;
But now, I wot not how it be,
You take me seldom on your knee,   10
Yet ne'ertheless I am right glad,
    To sit beside you, dad.

How lank and thin your beard hangs down!
Scant are the white hairs on your crown;
How wan and hollow are your cheeks!
Your brow is rough with crossing breaks;
But yet, for all his strength be fled,
    I love my own old dad.

The housewives round their potions brew,
And gossips come to ask for you;   20
And for your weal each neighbour cares,
And good men kneel, and say their prayers;

And everybody looks so sad,
    When you are ailing, dad.

You will not die and leave us then?
Rouse up and be our dad again.
When you are quiet and laid in bed,
We'll doff our shoes and softly tread;
And when you wake we'll aye be near
    To fill old dad his cheer.   30

When through the house you shift your stand,
I'll lead you kindly by the hand;
When dinner's set I'll with you bide,
And aye be serving at your side;
And when the weary fire burns blue,
    I'll sit and talk with you.

I have a tale both long and good,
About a partlet and her brood,
And cunning greedy fox that stole
By dead of midnight through a hole,   40
Which slyly to the hen-roost led –
    You love a story, dad?

And then I have a wondrous tale
Of men all clad in coats of mail,
With glittering swords – you nod, I think?
Your fixed eyes begin to wink;
Down on your bosom sinks your head –
    You do not hear me, dad.

THE KITTEN

Wanton droll, whose harmless play
Beguiles the rustic's closing day,
When, drawn the evening fire about,
Sit aged crone and thoughtless lout,
And child upon his three-foot stool,
Waiting till his supper cool,
And maid, whose cheek outblooms the rose,
As bright the blazing faggot glows,
Who, bending to the friendly light,
Plies her task with busy slight;   10
Come, show thy tricks and sportive graces,
Thus circled round with merry faces.

     Backward coiled and crouching low,
With glaring eyeballs watch thy foe,
The housewife's spindle whirling round,
Or thread or straw that on the ground
Its shadow throws, by urchin sly
Held out to lure thy roving eye;
Then stealing onward, fiercely spring
Upon the tempting faithless thing.   20
Now, wheeling round with bootless skill,
Thy bo-peep tail provokes thee still,
As still beyond thy curving side
Its jetty tip is seen to glide;
Till from thy centre starting far,
Thou sidelong veer'st with rump in air
Erected stiff, and gait awry,
Like madam in her tantrums high;
Though ne'er a madam of them all,
Whose silken kirtle sweeps the hall,   30
More varied trick and whim displays
To catch the admiring stranger's gaze.

     Doth power in measured verses dwell,
All thy vagaries wild to tell?
Ah no! – the start, the jet, the bound,
The giddy scamper round and round,
With leap and toss and high curvet,

And many a whirling somerset,
(Permitted by the modern muse
Expression technical to use)   40
These mock the deftest rhymester's skill,
But poor in art though rich in will.

　　　　The featest tumbler; stage bedight,
To thee is but a clumsy wight,
Who every limb and sinew strains
To do what costs thee little pains;
For which, I trow, the gaping crowd
Requite him oft with plaudits loud.

　　　　But, stopped the while thy wanton play,
Applauses too thy pains repay: 50
For then, beneath some urchin's hand
With modest pride thou takest thy stand,
While many a stroke of kindness glides
Along thy back and tabby sides.

SONG: 'O, WELCOME, BAT AND OWLET GRAY', WRITTEN FOR A WELSH AIR, CALLED 'THE PURSUIT OF LOVE'

O, welcome, bat and owlet gray,
Thus winging low your airy way!
And welcome, moth and drowsy fly,
That to mine ear comes humming by!
And welcome, shadows dim and deep,
And stars that through the pale sky peep!
O welcome all! to me ye say,
My woodland love is on her way.

Upon the soft wind floats her hair,
Her breath is in the dewy air;   10
Her steps are in the whispered sound
That steals along the stilly ground.

O dawn of day, in rosy bower,
What art thou to this witching hour?
O noon of day, in sunshine bright,
What art thou to the fall of night?

THE BLACK COCK:
WRITTEN FOR A WELSH AIR,
CALLED 'THE NOTE OF THE BLACK COCK'

Good morrow to thy sable beak,
And glossy plumage, dark and sleek,
Thy crimson moon and azure eye,
Cock of the heath, so wildly shy!
I see thee, slily cowering, through
That wiry web of silver dew,
That twinkles in the morning air,
Like casement of my lady fair.

A maid there is in yonder tower,
Who, peeping from her early bower,   10
Half shows, like thee, with simple wile,
Her braided hair and morning smile.
The rarest things with wayward will,
Beneath the covert hide them still:
The rarest things to light of day
Look shortly forth, and shrink away.

One fleeting moment of delight,
I sunned me in her cheering sight;
And short, I ween, the term will be,
That I shall parley hold with thee.   20
Through Snowden's mist red beams the day;
The climbing herdboy chaunts his lay;
The gnat-flies dance their sunny ring;
Thou art already on the wing.

SONG, WRITTEN FOR A WELSH MELODY:
'I'VE NO SHEEP ON THE MOUNTAIN'

I've no sheep on the mountain, nor boat on the lake,
Nor coin in my coffer to keep me awake,
Nor corn in my garner, nor fruit on my tree,
Yet the Maid of Llanwellyn smiles sweetly on me.

Softly tapping at eve on her window I came,
And loud bayed the watch-dog, loud scolded the dame;
For shame, silly Lightfoot! what is it to thee,
Though the Maid of Llanwellyn smiles sweetly on me.

The farmer rides proudly to market or fair,
The clerk at the alehouse still claims the great chair,   10
But, of all our proud fellows, the proudest I'll be,
While the Maid of Llanwellyn smiles sweetly on me?

For blithe as the urchin at holyday play,
And meek as a matron in mantle of gray,
And trim as a lady of gentle degree,
Is the Maid of Llanwellyn, who smiles upon me.

SONG,
WRITTEN FOR A WELSH AIR: 'NOH CALENIG'
OR 'THE NEW YEAR'S GIFT'

All white hang the bushes o'er Elaw's sweet stream,
And pale from the rock the long icicles gleam;
The first peep of morning just peers from the sky,
And here, at my door, gentle Mary, am I.

With the dawn of the year, and the dawn of the light,
The one who best loves thee stands first in thy sight,
Then welcome, dear maid! with my gift let me be –
A ribbon, a kiss, and a blessing for thee!

Last year, of earth's treasures I gave thee my part,
The new year before it, I gave thee my heart; 10
And now, gentle Mary, I greet thee again,
When only this band and a blessing remain.

Though Time should run on with his sack full of care,
And wrinkle thy cheek, dear, and whiten thy hair,
Yet still on this morn shall my offering be,
A ribbon, a kiss, and a blessing for thee.

SONG, WRITTEN AT MR THOMSON'S REQUEST: 'SWEET POWER OF SONG'

Sweet power of song! that canst impart
    To lowland swain or mountaineer
A gladness thrilling through the heart,
    A joy so tender and so dear!

Sweet power! that on a foreign strand
    Canst the rough soldier's bosom move
With feelings of his native land,
    As gentle as an infant's love!

Sweet power! that makest youthful heads,
    With thistle, leek or shamrock crowned, 10
Nod proudly as the carol sheds
    Its spirit through the social round!

Sweet power! that cheerest the daily toil
    Of cottage maid or beldame poor,
The ploughman on the furrowed soil,
    Or herd-boy on the lonely moor:

Or he by bards the Shepherd hight,
    Who mourns his maiden's broken tie,
Till the sweet plaint, in woe's despite,
    Hath made a bliss of agony: 20

Sweet power of song! thanks flow to thee
　　From every kind and gentle breast!
Let Erin's – Cambria's minstrels be
　　With Burns's tuneful spirit blest!

SONG,
WRITTEN FOR AN IRISH MELODY:
'HIS BOAT COMES ON THE SUNNY TIDE'

His boat comes on the sunny tide,
And briskly moves the flashing oar,
The boatmen carol by his side,
And blithely near the welcome shore.

How softly Shannon's currents flow,
His shadow in the stream I see;
The very waters seem to know,
Dear is the freight they bear to me.

His eager bound, his hasty tread,
His well-known voice I'll shortly hear;　　　　　　　　　10
And oh, those arms so kindly spread!
That greeting smile! That manly tear!

In other lands, when far away,
My love with hope did never twain;
I saw him thus, both night and day,
To Shannon's banks returned again.

SONG,
WRITTEN FOR AN IRISH MELODY:
'THE HARPER WHO SAT ON HIS GREEN MOSSY SEAT'

The harper who sat on his green mossy seat,
And harped to the youngsters so loud and so sweet,
The far distant hum of the children at play,
And the maiden's soft carol at close of the day –

Ah! this was the music delighted my ear,
And to think of it now is so sad and so dear!
Ah! to listen again, by mine own cottage door,
To the sound of mine own native village once more!

I knew every dame in her holy-day airs;
I knew every maiden that danced at our fairs;   10
I knew every farmer to market who came,
And the dog that ran after him called by its name.

And who know I now in this far distant land,
But the stiff-collared sergeant, and red-coated band?
No kinsman to comfort his own flesh and blood;
No merry-eyed damsel to do my heart good!

To mine eye or mine ear no gay cheering e'er comes,
But the flare of our colours, the tuck of our drums;
The fierce flashing steel of our long-mustered file,
And the sharp shrilly fifers a-playing the while.   20

At night, as I keep on the wearisome watch,
The sound of the west wind I greedily catch,
Then the shores of dear Ireland will rise to my sight,
And mine own native valley, that spot of delight!

Divided so far by a wide stormy main
Shall I ever return to our valley again?
Ah! to listen at ease by mine own cottage door,
To the sound of mine own native village once more!

SONG,
FOR AN IRISH AIR:
'THE MORNING AIR PLAYS ON MY FACE'

The morning air plays on my face,
And through the grey mist peering
The softened sun I sweetly trace,
Wood, muir and mountain cheering.
      Larks aloft are singing,
      Hares from covert springing,
And o'er the fen the wild-duck brood
      Their early way are winging.

Bright every dewy hawthorn shines,
Sweet every herb is growing,   10
To him whose willing heart inclines
The way that he is going.
      Clearly do I see now
      What will shortly be now;
I'm patting at her door poor Tray,
      Who fawns and welcomes me now.

How slowly moves the rising latch!
How quick my heart is beating!
That worldly dame is on the watch
To frown upon our meeting.   20
      Fy! why should I mind her,
      See who stands behind her,
Whose eye upon her traveller looks
      The sweeter and the kinder.

O every bounding step I take,
Each hour the clock is telling,
Bears me o'er mountain, bourn and brake
Still nearer to her dwelling.
      Day is shining brighter.
      Limbs are moving lighter,   30
While every thought to Nora's love,
      But bind my love the tighter.

SONG,
FOR AN IRISH AIR:
'COME, FORM WE ROUND A CHEERFUL RING'

Come, form we round a cheerful ring
    And broach the foaming ale,
And let the merry maiden sing,
    The beldame tell her tale.

And let the sightless harper sit
    The blazing faggot near;
And let the jester vent his wit,
    The nurse her bantling cheer.

Who shakes the door with angry din,
    And would admitted be?   10
No, Gossip Winter! snug within,
    We have no room for thee.

Go scud it o'er Killarney's lake,
    And shake the willows bare,
Where water-elves their pastime take,
    Thou'lt find thy comrades there.

Will-o'-the-wisp skips in the dell,
    The owl hoots on the tree,
They hold their nightly vigil well,
    And so the while will we.   20

Then strike we up the rousing glee,
    And pass the beaker round,
Till every head, right merrily
    Is moving to the sound.

SONG:
'COME ROUSE THEE, LADY FAIR'

Come rouse thee, lady fair,
    The sun is shining brightly,
High through the cloudless air
    The sea-bird roving lightly.

Come from thy lattice look;
    With many an oar in motion,
Boats have the creek forsook,
    And course the azure ocean.

See on the dim waves borne,
    White distant sails are gliding;   10
Good, on so fair a morn,
    In every heart abiding.

SONG:
FOR FISHERMEN

The waves are rippling on the sand,
    The winds are still, the air is clear;
Then gather round, my merry band,
    We'll hold on shore an hour of cheer!

The lord keeps vigil in his hall,
    The dame in bower or turret high;
But meet the merriest mates of all
    Beneath the summer's starlight sky!

SONG,
FOR MR STRUTHER'S *THE HARP OF CALEDONIA*:
'IT WAS ON A MORN, WHEN WE WERE THRANG'

It was on a morn, when we were thrang,
  The kirn it crooned, the cheese was making,
And bannocks on the girdle baking,
  When ane at the door chapp't loud and lang.

Yet the auld gudewife and her mays sae tight,
  Of a' this bald din took sma' notice I ween;
For a chap at the door in braid day-light,
  Is no like a chap that's heard at e'en.

But the docksy auld laird of the Warlock glen,
  Wha waited without, half blate, half cheery,   10
And lang'd for a sight o' his winsome deary,
  Raised up the latch, and cam' crously ben.

His coat it was new, and his o'erlay was white,
  His mittens and hose were cozy and bien;
But a wooer that comes in braid daylight,
  Is no like a wooer that comes at e'en.

He greeted the carline and lasses sae braw,
  And his bare liart pow, sae smoothly he straikit,
And he looket about, like a body half glaikit,
  On bonny sweet Nanny the youngest of a'.   20

'Ha laird!' quo' the carline, 'and look ye that way?
  Fy, let na' sic fancies bewilder ye clean:
An elderlin man, in the noon o' the day,
  Should be wiser than youngsters that come at e'en.'

'Na, na,' quo' the pawky auld wife, 'I trow,
  You'll no fash you head wi' a youthfu' gilly,
As wild and as skeigh as a muirland filly;
  Black Madge is far better and fitter for you.'

He hem'd and he haw'd, and he drew in his mouth,
    And he squeezed the blue bannet his twa hands between,   30
For a wooer that comes when the sun's i' the south,
    Is mair landward than wooers that come at e'en.

'Black Madge is sae carefu'' – 'What's that to me?
    'She's sober and ident, has sense in her noddle;
She's douce and respeckit' – 'I care na' a bodle,
    Love winna be guided, and fancy's free.'

Madge tossed back her head wi' a saucy slight,
    And Nanny, loud laughing, ran out to the green;
For a wooer that comes when the sun shines bright,
    Is no like a wooer that comes at e'en.   40

The awa flung the Laird, and loud muttered he,
    'A' the daughters of Eve, between Orkney and Tweed o!
Black or fair, young or auld, dame or damsel or widow,
    May gang in their pride to the de'il for me!'

But the auld gudewife and her mays sae tight
    Cared little for a' his stour banning, I ween;
For a wooer that comes in braid daylight,
    Is no' like a wooer that comes at e'en.

TO A CHILD

Whose imp art thou, with dimpled cheek,
    And curly pate and merry eye,
And arm and shoulders round and sleek,
    And soft and fair? thou urchin sly!

What boots it who, with sweet caresses,
    First called thee his, or squire or hind? –
For thou in every wight that passes,
    Dost now a friendly playmate find.

Thy downcast glances, grave but cunning,
　　As fringed eyelids rise and fall,　　　　　　　　10
Thy shyness, swiftly from me running –
　　'Tis infantine coquetry all!

But far afield thou hast not flown,
　　With mocks and threats half-lisped half-spoken,
I feel thee pulling at my gown,
　　Of right goodwill thy simple token.

And thou must laugh and wrestle too,
　　A mimic warfare with me waging,
To make, as wily lovers do,
　　Thy after-kindness more engaging.　　　　　　　20

The wilding rose, sweet as thyself,
　　And new-cropped daisies are thy treasure,
I'd gladly part with worldly pelf,
　　To taste again thy youthful pleasure.

But yet for all thy merry look,
　　Thy frisks and wiles, the time is coming,
When thou shalt sit in cheerless nook,
　　The weary spell or hornbook thumbing.

Well; let it be! thro' weal and woe,
　　Thou knowest not now thy future range;　　　　30
Life is a motley shifting show,
　　And thou a thing of hope and change.

SONG, WOO'D AND MARRIED AND A'
(VERSION TAKEN FROM AN OLD SONG OF THAT NAME)

The bride she is winsome and bonny,
    Her hair it is snooded sae sleek,
And faithfu' and kind is her Johnny,
    Yet fast fa' the tears on her cheek.
New pearlins are cause of her sorrow,
    New pearlins and plenishing too,
The bride that has a' to borrow,
    Has e'en right mickle ado.
        Woo'd and married and a'!
        Woo'd and married and a'!   10
      Is na' she very weel aff
        To be woo'd and married at a'?

Her mither then hastily spak,
    'The lassie is glakit wi' pride;
In my pouch I had never a plack
    On the day when I was a bride.
E'en tak' to your wheel, and be clever,
    And draw out your thread in the sun;
The gear that is gifted, it never
    Will last like the gear that is won.   20
        Woo'd and married and a'!
        Wi' havins and tocher sae sma'!
      I think ye are very weel aff,
        To be woo'd and married at a'!'

'Toot, toot!' quo' her grey-headed faither,
    'She's less o' a bride than a bairn,
She's ta'en like a cout frae the heather,
    Wi' sense and discretion to learn.
Half husband, I trow, and half daddy,
    As humour inconstantly leans,   30
The chiel maun be patient and steady,
     That yokes wi' a mate in her teens.
        A kerchief sae douce and sae neat,
        O'er her locks that the winds used to blaw!
      I'm baith like to laugh and to greet,
        When I think o' her married at a'!'

Then out spak' the wily bridegroom,
 Weel waled were his wordies, I ween,
'I'm rich, though my coffer be toom,
 Wi' the blinks o' your bonny blue een. 40
I'm prouder o' thee by my side,
 Though thy ruffles or ribbons be few,
Than if Kate o' the Croft were my bride,
 Wi' purfles and pearlins enow.
  Dear, and dearest of ony!
  Ye're woo'd and buikit and a'!
 And do ye think scorn o' your Johnny,
  And grieve to be married at a'?'

She turned, and she blushed, and she smiled,
 And she looket sae bashfully down; 50
The pride o' her heart was beguiled,
 And she played wi' the sleeves o' her gown;
She twirled the tag o' her lace,
 And she nippet her boddice sae blue,
Syne blinket sae sweet in his face,
 And aff like a maukin she flew.
  Woo'd and married and a'!
  Wi' Johnny to roose her and a'!
 She thinks hersel very weel aff,
  To be woo'd and married at a'. 60

A NOVEMBER NIGHT'S TRAVELLER

He, who with journey well begun,
Beneath the beam of morning's sun,
Stretching his view o'er hill and dale,
And distant city, (thro' its veil
Of smoke, dark spires and chimneys showing,)
O'er harvest-lands with plenty flowing,
What time the roused and busy, meeting
On King's highway, exchange their greeting, –
Feels his cheered heart with pleasure beat,
As on his way he holds. And great 10

Delight hath he, who travels late,
What time the moon doth hold her state
In the clear sky, while down and dale
Repose in light so pure and pale! –
While lake and pool and stream are seen
Weaving their maze of silvery sheen, –
While cot and mansion, rock and glade,
And tower and street, in light and shade
Strongly contrasted, are, I trow!
Grander than aught of noon-day show,   20
Soothing the pensive mind.

                And yet,
When moon is dark, and sun is set,
Not reft of pleasure is the wight,
Who, in snug chaise, at close of night
Begins his journey in the dark,
With crack of whip and ban-dog's bark,
And jarring wheels, and children bawling,
And voice of surly ostler, calling
To post-boy, thro' the mingled din,
Some message to a neighbouring inn,   30
Which sound confusedly in his ear;
The lonely way's commencing cheer.

        With dull November's starless sky
O'er head, his fancy soars not high.
The carriage lamps a white light throw
Along the road, and strangely show
Familiar things which cheat the eyes,
Like friends in motley masker's guise.
'What's that? or dame, or mantled maid,
Or herdboy gathered in his plaid,   40
Which leans against yon wall his back?
No; 'tis in sooth a tiny stack
Of turf or peat, or rooty wood,
For cottage fire the winter's food. –'
        'Ha! yonder shady nook discovers
A gentle pair of rustic lovers.
Out on't! A pair of harmless calves,
Thro' straggling bushes seen by halves. –'

'What thing of strange unshapely height
Approaches slowly on the light,   50
That like a hunch-backed giant seems,
And now is whitening in its beams?
'Tis but a hind, whose burly back
Is bearing home a loaded sack. –'
        'What's that, like spots of fleckered snow,
Which on the road's wide margin show?
'Tis linen left to bleach by night.'
            'Grammercy on us! see I right?
Some witch is casting cantrips there;
The linen hovers in the air! –   60
Pooh! Soon or late all wonders cease,
We have but scared a flock of geese. –'
        Thus oft through life we do misdeem
Of things that are not what they seem.
Ah! could we there with as slight skathe
Divest us of our cheated faith!
        And then belike, when chiming bells
The near approach of waggon tells,
He wistful looks to see it come,
Its bulk emerging from the gloom,   70
With dun tarpaulin o'er it thrown,
Like a huge mammoth, moving on.
        But yet more pleased, thro' murky air
He spies the distant bonfire's glare;
And, nearer to the spot advancing,
Black imps and goblins round it dancing;
And, nearer still, distinctly traces
The featured disks of happy faces,
Grinning and roaring in their glory,
Like Bacchants wild of ancient story,   80
And making murgeons to the flame,
As *it* were playmate of their game.
Full well, I think, could modern stage
Such acting for the nonce engage,
A crowded audience every night
Would press to see the jovial sight;
And this, from cost and squeezing free,
November's nightly travellers see.

              Thro' village, lane, or hamlet going,
The light from cottage window showing   90
Its inmates at their evening fare,
By rousing fire, and earthenware –
And pewter trenchers on the shelf, –
Harmless displays of worldly pelf! –
Is transient vision to the eye
Of hasty traveller passing by;
Yet much of pleasing import tells,
And cherished in the fancy dwells,
Where simple innocence and mirth
Encircles still the cottage hearth.   100
Across the road a fiery glare
Doth blacksmith's open forge declare,
Where furnace-blast, and measured din
Of hammers twain, and all within, –
The brawny mates their labour plying,
From heated bar the red sparks flying,
And idle neighbours standing by
With open mouth and dazzled eye,
The rough and sooty walls with store
Of chains and horse-shoes studded o'er, –   110
An armoury of sullied sheen, –
All momently are heard and seen,

              Nor does he often fail to meet,
In market town's dark narrow street,
(Even when the night on pitchy wings
The sober hour of bedtime brings,)
Amusement. From the alehouse door,
Having full bravely paid his score,
Issues the tipsy artisan,
With tipsier brother of the can,   120
And oft to wile him homeward tries
With coaxing words, so wondrous wise!
        The dame demure, from visit late,
Her lantern borne before in state
By sloven footboy, paces slow,
With pattened feet and hooded brow.
              Where the seamed window-board betrays
Interior light, full closely lays

The eavesdropper his curious ear,
Some neighbour's fireside talk to hear;   130
While, from an upper casement bending,
A household maid, belike, is sending
From jug or ewer a sloppy shower,
That makes him homeward fleetly scour.
From lower rooms few gleams are sent,
From blazing hearth, thro' chink or rent;
But from the loftier chambers peer
(Where damsels doff their gentle gear,
For rest preparing,) tapers bright,
Which give a momentary sight   140
Of some fair form with visage glowing,
With loosened braids and tresses flowing,
Who, busied, by the mirror stands,
With bending head and upraised hands,
Whose moving shadow strangely falls
With size enlarged on roof and walls.
Ah! lovely are the things, I ween,
By arrowy Speed's light glamoury seen!
Fancy, so touched, will long retain
That quickly seen, nor seen again.   150

But now he spies the flaring door
Of bridled Swan or gilded Boar,
At which the bowing waiter stands
To know th'alighting guest's commands.
A place of bustle, dirt, and din,
Cursing without, scolding within;
Of narrow means and ample boast,
The traveller's stated halting post,
Where trunks are missing or deranged,
And parcels lost and horses changed.   160

Yet this short scene of noisy coil
But serves our traveller as a foil,
Enhancing what succeeds, and lending
A charm to pensive quiet, sending
To home and friends, left far behind,
The kindliest musings of his mind;
Or, should they stray to thoughts of pain,

A dimness o'er the haggard train
A mood and hour like this will throw,
As vexed and burthened spirits know.   170

      Night, loneliness, and motion are
Agents of power to distance care;
To distance, not discard; for then,
Withdrawn from busy haunts of men,
Necessity to act suspended,
The present, past, and future blended,
Like figures of a mazy dance,
Weave round the soul a dreamy trance,
Till jolting stone, or turnpike gate,
Arouse him from the soothing state.   180

      And when the midnight hour is past,
If thro' the night his journey last,
When still and lonely is the road,
Nor living creature moves abroad,
Then most of all, like fabled wizard,
Night slily dons her cloak and vizard,
His eyes at every corner greeting,
With some new slight of dexterous cheating,
And cunningly his sight betrays,
Even with his own lamps' partial rays.   190

      The road, that in fair simple day
Through pasture-land or corn-fields lay,
A broken hedge-row's ragged screen
Skirting its weedy margin green, –
With boughs projecting, interlaced
With thorn and briar, distinctly traced
On the deep shadows at their back,
That deeper sink to pitchy black,
Appearing oft to Fancy's eye,
Like woven boughs of tapestry, –   200
Seems now to wind through tangled wood
Or forest wild, where Robin Hood,
With all his outlaws, stout and bold,
In olden days his reign might hold,
Where vagrant school-boy fears to roam,

The gypsy's chant, the woodman's home.
     Yes, roofless barn and ruined wall,
As passing lights upon them fall,
When favoured by surrounding gloom,
The castle's ruined state assume.   210
     The steamy vapour that proceeds
From moistened hide of weary steeds,
And high on either hand doth rise,
Like clouds, storm-drifted, past him flies;
While liquid mire, by their hoofed feet
Cast up, adds magic to the cheat,
Glancing presumptuously before him,
Like yellow diamonds of Cairngorm.

     How many are the subtle ways,
By which sly Night the eye betrays,   220
When in her wild fantastic mood,
By lone and wakeful traveller wooed!
Shall I proceed? O no! for now
Upon the black horizon's brow
Appears a line of tawny light;
Thy reign is ended, witching Night!
And soon thy place a wizard elph,
(But only second to thyself
In glamourie's art) will quietly take,
Spreading o'er meadow, vale, and brake,   230
Her misty shroud of pearly white:
A modest, though deceitful wight,
Who in a softer, gentler way,
Will with the wakeful fancy play,
When knolls of woods, their bases losing,
Are islands on a lake reposing,
And streeted town, of high pretence,
As rolls away the vapour dense,
With all its wavy curling billows,
Is but a row of pollard willows: 240
O no! my traveller, still and lone,
A far fatiguing way hath gone;
His eyes are dim, he stoops his crest,
And folds his arms, and goes to rest.

ADDRESS TO A STEAM-VESSEL

Freighted with passengers of every sort,
A motley throng, thou leavest the busy port.
Thy long and ample deck, where scattered lie,
Baskets, and cloaks, and shawls of scarlet dye;
Where dogs and children through the crowd are straying,
And, on his bench apart, the fiddler playing,
While matron dames to tresselled seats repair,
Seems, on the gleamy waves, a floating fair.

    Its dark form on the sky's pale azure cast,
Towers from this clustering group thy pillared mast.   10
The dense smoke issuing from its narrow vent
Is to the air in curly volumes sent,
Which, coiling and uncoiling on the wind,
Trails like a writhing serpent far behind.
Beneath, as each merged wheel its motion plies,
On either side the white-churned waters rise,
And, newly parted from the noisy fray,
Track with light ridgy foam thy recent way,
Then far diverged, in many a welted line
Of lustre, on the distant surface shine.   20

    Thou holdest thy course in independent pride;
No leave asked thou of either wind or tide.
To whate'er point the breeze, inconstant, veer,
Still doth thy careless helmsman onward steer;
As if the stroke of some magician's wand
Had lent thee power the ocean to command.
What is this power which thus within thee lurks,
And, all unseen, like a masked giant works?
Even that which gentle dames, at morning's tea
From silver urn ascending, daily see   30
With tressy wreathings playing in the air,
Like the loosed ringlets of a lady's hair;
Or rising from the enamelled cup beneath,
With the soft fragrance of an infant's breath:
That which within the peasant's humble cot
Comes from the uncovered mouth of savoury pot,
As his kind mate prepares his noonday fare,

Which cur, and cat, and rosy urchins share:
That which, all silvered with the moon's pale beam,
Precedes the mighty Geyser's upcast stream,   40
What time, with bellowing din exploded forth,
It decks the midnight of the frozen north,
Whilst travellers from their skin-spread couches rise
To gaze upon the sight with wondering eyes.

     Thou hast to those 'in populous city pent'
Glimpses of wild and beauteous nature lent;
A bright remembrance ne'er to be destroyed,
Which proves to them a treasure, long enjoyed,
And for this scope to beings erst confined,
I fain would hail thee with a grateful mind.   50
They who had nought of verdant freshness seen
But suburb orchards choked with colworts green,
Now, seated at their ease may glide along,
Loch Lomond's fair and fairy isles among;
Where bushy promontories fondly peep,
At their own beauty in the nether deep,
O'er drooping birch and berried rowan that lave
Their fragrant branches in the glassy wave:
They, who on higher objects scarce have counted
Than church's spire with gilded vane surmounted,   60
May view, within their near, distinctive ken,
The rocky summits of the lofty Ben;
Or see his purpled shoulders darkly lower
Through the dim drapery of a summer shower.
Where, spread in broad and fair expanse, the Clyde
Mingles his waters with the briny tide,
Along the lesser Cumra's rocky shore,
With moss and crusted lichens fleckered o'er.
Even he, who hath but warred with thieving cat,
Or from his cupboard chased a hungry rat,   70
The city cobbler, – scares the wild sea-mew
In its mid-flight with loud and shrill halloo;
Or valiantly with fearful threatening shakes
His lank and greasy head at Kittywakes.
The eyes that have no fairer outline seen
Than chimneyed walls with slated roofs between,
Which hard and harshly edge the smokey sky;

May Arran's softly-visioned peaks descry,
Coping with graceful states her steepy sides,
O'er which the cloud's broad shadow softly glides,   80
And interlacing slopes that gently merge
Into the pearly mist of ocean's verge.
Eyes which admired that work of sordid skill,
The storied structure of a cotton-mill,
May, wondering, now behold the unnumbered host
Of marshalled pillars on fair Ireland's coast,
Phalanx on phalanx ranged with sidelong bend,
Or broken ranks that to the main descend,
Like Pharaoh's army, on the Red Sea shore,
Which deep and deeper went to rise no more.   90

          Yet, ne'ertheless, whate'er we owe to thee,
Rover at will on river, lake, and sea,
As profit's bait or pleasure's lure engage,
Thou offspring of that philosophic sage,
Watt, who in heraldry of science ranks
With those to whom men owe high meed of thanks,
And shall not be forgotten, even when Fame
Graves on her annals Davy's splendid name!
Dearer to fancy, to the eye more fair
Are the light skiffs, that to the breezy air,   100
Unfurl their swelling sails of snowy hue
Upon the moving lap of ocean blue.
As the proud swan on summer lake displays,
With plumage brightening in the morning rays,
Her fair pavilion of erected wings,
They change, and veer, and turn like living things.

          So fairly rigged, with shrouding, sails and mast,
To brave with manly skill the winter blast
Of every clime – in vessels rigged like these
Did great Columbus cross the western seas,   110
And to the stinted thoughts of man revealed
What yet the course of ages had concealed.
In such as these, on high adventure bent,
Round the vast world Magellan's comrades went.
To such as these are hardy seamen found
As with the ties of kindred feeling bound,

Boasting, as cans of cheering grog they sip,
The varied fortunes of 'our gallant ship'.
The offspring these of bold sagacious man
Ere yet the reign of lettered lore began.   120

       In very truth, compared to these thou art
A daily labourer, a mechanic swart,
In working weeds arrayed of homely grey,
Opposed to gentle nymph or lady gay,
To whose free robes the graceful right is given
To play and dally with the winds of heaven.
Beholding thee, the great of other days
And modern men with all their altered ways,
Across my mind with hasty transit gleam,
Like fleeting shadows of a feverish dream: 130
Fitful I gaze with adverse humours teased,
Half sad, half proud, half angry, and half pleased.

SIR MAURICE, A BALLAD

Sir Maurice was a wealthy lord,
   He lived in the north country,
Well could he cope with foeman's sword,
   Or the glance of a lady's eye.

Now all his armed vassals wait,
   A staunch and burly band,
Before his stately castle's gate,
   Bound for the Holy Land.

Above the spearmen's lengthened file,
   Are figured ensigns flying;   10
Stroked by their keeper's hand the while,
   Are harnessed chargers neighing.

And looks of woe and looks of cheer,
    And looks the two between,
On many a warlike face appear,
    Where tears have lately been.

For all they love is left behind;
    Hope beckons them before:
Their parting sails spread to the wind,
    Blown from their native shore.   20

Then thro' the crowded portal passed
    Six goodly knights and tall;
Sir Maurice himself, who came the last,
    Was goodliest of them all.

And proudly roved his hasty eye
    O'er all the warlike train;
'Save ye, brave comrades, prosperously,
    Heaven send us o'er the main!

But see I right? An armed band
    From Moorham's lordless hall;   30
And he who bears the high command,
    Its ancient seneschal!

Return; your stately keep defend;
    Defend your lady's bower,
Lest rude and lawless hands should rend,
    That lone and lovely flower.'

'God will defend our lady dear,
    And we will cross the sea,
From slavery's chain, his lot severe,
    Our noble lord to free.'   40

'Nay, nay! Some wandering minstrel's tongue,
    Hath framed a story vain;
Thy lord, his liegemen brave among,
    Near Acre's wall was slain.'

'Nay, good my lord! for had his life
   Been lost on battle-ground,
When ceased that fell and fatal strife,
   His body had been found.'

'No faith to such delusions give;
   His mortal term is past.'   50
'Not so! Not so! He is alive,
   And will be found at last!'

These latter words right eagerly,
   From a slender stripling broke,
Who stood the ancient warrior by,
   And trembled as he spoke.

Sir Maurice started at the sound,
   And all from top to toe
The stripling scanned, who to the ground
   His blushing face bent low.   60

'Is this thy kinsman, seneschal?
   Thine own or thy sister's son?
A gentler page, in tent or hall,
   Mine eyes ne'er looked upon.

To thine own fair home return, fair youth!
   To thine own home return.
Give ear to likely, sober truth.
   Nor prudent counsel spurn.

War suits thee not, if boy thou art;
   And if a sweeter name   70
Befit thee, do not lightly part
   With maiden's honoured fame.'

He turned him from his liegeman all,
   Who round their chieftain pressed;
His very shadow on the wall
   His troubled mind expressed.

As sometimes slow and sometimes fast,
   He paced to and fro,
His plumy crest now upward cast
   In air, now drooping low.   80

Sometimes like one in frantic mood,
   Short words of sound he uttered,
And sometimes, stopping short, he stood,
   As to himself he muttered.

'A daughter's love, a maiden's pride!
   And may they not agree?
Could man desire a lovelier bride,
   A truer friend than she?

Down, cursed thought! A boy's garb
   Betrays not wanton will,   90
Yet, sharper than an arrow's barb,
   That fear might haunt me still.'

He muttered long, then to the gate,
   Returned and looked around,
But the seneschal and his stripling mate
   Were nowhere to be found.

With outward cheer and inward smart,
   In warlike fair array,
Did Maurice with his bands depart,
   And shoreward bent his way.   100

Their stately ship rode near the port,
   The warriors to receive,
And there, with blessings kind but short,
   Did friends of friends take leave.

And soon they saw the crowded strand
   Wear dimly from their view,
And soon they saw the distant land,
   A line of hazy blue.

The white-sailed ship with favouring breeze,
    In all her gallant pride, 110
Moved like the mistress of the seas,
    That rippled far and wide.

Sometimes with steady course she went,
    O'er wave and surge careering,
Sometimes with sidelong mast she bent,
    Her wings the sea-foam sheering.

Sometimes, with poles and rigging bare,
    She scudded before the blast,
But safely by the Syrian shore,
    Her anchor dropped at last. 120

What martial honours Maurice won,
    Joined with the brave and great,
From the fierce, faithless Saracen,
    I may not here relate.

With boldest band on bridge or moat,
    With a champion on the plain,
In the breach with clustering foes he fought,
    Choked up with grisly slain.

Most valiant by the valiant styled,
    Their praise his deeds proclaimed, 130
And oft his liegemen proudly smiled
    To hear their leader named.

But fate will quell the hero's strength,
    And dim the loftiest brow,
And this, our noble chief, at length
    Was in the dust laid low.

He lay the heaps of dead beneath,
    As sunk life's flickering flame,
And thought it was the trance of death,
    That o'er his senses came. 140

And when again day's blessed light
   Did on his vision fall,
There stood by his side, a wondrous sight!
   The ancient seneschal.

He strove, but could not utter word,
   His misty senses fled;
Again he woke, and Moorham's lord
   Was bending o'er his bed.

A third time sank he, as if dead,
   And then, his eyelids raising,   150
He saw a chief with turbaned head,
   Intently on him gazing.

'The prophet's zealous servant I;
   His battles I've fought and won;
Christians I scorn, their creeds deny,
   But honour Mary's son.

And I have wedded an English dame,
   And set her parent free;
And none, who wears an English name,
   Shall e'er be thralled by me.   160

For her dear sake I can endure
   All wrong, all hatred smother;
Whate'er I feel, thou art secure,
   As tho' thou wert my brother.'

'And thou hast wedded an English dame!'
   Sir Maurice said no more,
For o'er his heart a weakness came,
   He sighed and wept full sore.

And many a dreary day and night
   With the Moslem chief stayed he,   170
But ne'er could catch, to bless his sight,
   One glimpse of the fair lady.

Oft gazed he on her lattice high
  As he paced the court below,
And turned his listening ear to try
  If word or accent low

Might haply reach him there; and oft
  Traversed the garden green,
Wotting her footsteps small and soft
  Might on the turf be seen.   180

And oft to Moorham's lord he gave
  His listening ear, who told,
How he became a wretched slave
  Within that Syrian hold;

What time from liegemen parted far,
  Upon the battlefield,
By stern and adverse fate of war
  He was obliged to yield:

And how his daughter did by stealth
  So boldly cross the sea   190
With secret store of gathered wealth,
  To set her father free:

And how into the foeman's hands
  She and her people fell;
And how (herself in captive bands)
  She sought him in his cell;

And but a captive boy appeared,
  Till grief her sex betrayed,
And the fierce Saracen, so feared!
  Spoke gently to the maid: 200

How for her plighted hand sued he,
  And solemn promise gave,
Her noble father should be free
  With every Christian slave;

(For many there, in bondage kept,
    Felt the stern rule of vice;)
How, long she pondered, sorely wept,
    Then paid the fearful price. –

A tale which made his bosom thrill,
    His faded eyes to weep;   210
He, waking, thought upon it still,
    And saw it in his sleep.

But harness rings, and the trumpet's bray
    Again to battle calls;
And Christian powers, in grand array,
    Are near those Moslem walls.

Sir Maurice heard; untoward fate!
    Sad to be thought upon:
But the castle's lord unlocked its gate,
    And bade his guest be gone.   220

'Fight thou for faith by thee adored;
    By thee so well maintained!
But never may this trusty sword
    With blood of thine be stained!' –

Sir Maurice took him by the hand,
    'God bless thee too,' he cried;
Then to the nearest Christian band
    With mingled feelings hied.

The battle joined, with dauntless pride
    'Gainst foemen, foemen stood;   230
And soon the fatal field was dyed
    With many a brave man's blood.

At length gave way the Moslem force;
    Their valiant chief was slain;
Maurice protected his lifeless corpse,
    And bore it from the plain.

There's mourning in the Moslem halls,
   A dull and dismal sound:
The lady left its 'leaguered walls,
   And safe protection found. 240

When months were past, the widowed dame
   Looked calm and cheerfully;
Then Maurice to her presence came,
   And bent him on his knee.

What words of penitence or suit
   He uttered, pass we by;
The lady wept, a while was mute,
   Then gave this firm reply:

'That thou didst doubt my maiden pride
   (A thought that rose and vanished 250
So fleetingly) I will not chide;
   'Tis from remembrance banished.

But thy fair fame, earned by that sword,
   Still spotless shall it be:
I was the bride of a Moslem lord,
   And will never be bride to thee.'

So firm, though gentle, was her look,
   Hope in the instant fled;
A solemn, dear farewell he took,
   And from her presence sped. 260

And she a plighted nun became,
   God serving day and night;
And he of blest Jerusalem
   A brave and zealous knight.

But that their lot was one of woe,
   Wot ye, because of this
Their separate single state? If so,
   In sooth ye judge amiss.

She tends the helpless stranger's bed,
   For alms her wealth is stored;   270
On her meek worth God's grace is shed,
   Man's grateful blessings poured.

He still in warlike mail doth stalk,
   In arms his prowess prove;
And oft of siege or battle talk,
   And sometimes of his love.

She was the fairest of the fair,
   The gentlest of the kind;
Search ye the wide world everywhere,
   Her like ye shall not find.   280

She *was* the fairest, *is* the best,
   Too good for a monarch's bride;
I would not give her in her nun's coif dressed
   For all her sex beside.

TO MRS SIDDONS

Gifted of Heaven! who hast, in days gone by,
Moved every heart, delighted every eye;
While age and youth, of high and low degree,
In sympathy were joined, beholding thee,
As in the drama's ever changing scene,
Thou held'st thy splendid state, our tragic queen!
No barriers there thy fair domains confined,
Thy sovereign sway was o'er the human mind;
And, in the triumph of that witching hour,
Thy lofty bearing well became thy power.   10

  The impassioned changes of thy beauteous face,
Thy stately form, and high imperial grace;
Thine arms impetuously tossed, thy robe's wide flow,

And the dark tempest gathered on thy brow;
What time thy flashing eye and lip of scorn,
Down to the dust thy mimic foes have borne;
Remorseful musings, sunk to deep dejection,
The fixed and yearning looks of strong affection;
The active turmoil of a bosom rending,
When pity, love, and honour, are contending;   20
They who beheld all this, right well, I ween,
A lovely, grand, and wondrous sight have seen.

    Thy varied accents, rapid, fitful, slow,
Loud rage, and fear's snatched whisper, quick and low;
The burst of stifled love, the wail of grief,
And tones of high command, full, solemn, brief;
The change of voice, and emphasis that threw
Light on obscurity, and brought to view
Distinctions nice, when grave or comic mood,
Or mingled humours, terse and new, elude   30
Common perception, as earth's smallest things
To size and form, the vesting hoar-frost brings,
That seemed as if some secret voice, to clear
The ravelled meaning, whispered in thine ear,
And thou hadst even with him communion kept,
Who hath so long in Stratford's chancel slept;
Whose lines, where nature's brightest traces shine,
Alone were worthy deemed of powers like thine:
They who have heard all this, have proved full well
Of soul-exciting sound, the mightiest spell.   40

    But though time's lengthened shadows o'er thee glide,
And pomp of regal state is cast aside,
Think not the glory of thy course is spent,
There's moonlight radiance to thy evening lent,
That, to the mental world can never fade,
Till all who have seen thee, in the grave are laid.
Thy graceful form still moves in nightly dreams,
And what thou wert, to the lulled sleeper seems:
While feverish fancy oft doth fondly trace
Within her curtained couch thy wondrous face.   50
Yea; and to many a wight, bereft and lone,
In musing hours, though all to thee unknown,

Soothing his earthly course of good and ill,
With all thy potent charm, thou actest still.

   And now in crowded room or rich saloon,
Thy stately presence recognized, how soon
On thee the glance of many an eye is cast,
In grateful memory of pleasures past!
Pleased to behold thee, with becoming grace,
Take, as befits thee well, an honoured place   60
(Where blest by many a heart, long mayest thou stand)
Among the virtuous matrons of our land.

HOOLY AND FAIRLY
(FOUNDED ON AN OLD SCOTTISH SONG)

Oh, neighbours! what had I a-do for to marry!
My wife she drinks posset and wine o' Canary,
And ca's me a niggardly, thraw-gabbit cairly,
   O, gin my wife wad drink hooly and fairly!
      Hooly and fairly, hooly and fairly,
   O, gin my wife wad drink hooly and fairly!

She sups wi' her kimmers on dainties enow,
Aye bowing and smirking and wiping her mou'
While I sit aside, and am helpit but sparely,
   O, gin my wife wad feast hooly and fairly!   10
      Hooly and fairly, hooly and fairly,
   O, gin my wife wad feast hooly and fairly!

To fairs and to bridals and preachings and a',
She gangs sae light headed and buskit sae braw,
In ribbons and mantuas that gar me gae barely!
   O, gin my wife wad spend hooly and fairly!
      Hooly and fairly, hooly and fairly,
   O, gin my wife wad spend hooly and fairly!

I' the kirk sic commotion last Sabbath she made,
Wi' babs o' red roses and breast-knots o'erlaid! 20
The Dominie stickit the psalm very nearly:
    O, gin my wife wad dress hooly and fairly!
        Hooly and fairly, hooly and fairly,
    O, gin my wife wad dress hooly and fairly!

She's warring and flyting frae morning till e'en,
And if ye gainsay her, her een glow'r sae keen,
Then tongue, nieve, and cudgel she'll lay on ye sairly:
    O, gin my wife wad strike hooly and fairly!
        Hooly and fairly, hooly and fairly,
    O, gin my wife wad strike hooly and fairly! 30

When tired wi' her cantrips, she lies in her bed,
The wark a' negleckit, the chaumer unred,
While a' our guid neighbours are stirring sae early:
    O, gin my wife wad wurk timely and fairly!
        Hooly and fairly, hooly and fairly,
    O, gin my wife wad wurk timely and fairly!

A word o' guid counsel or grace she'll hear none;
She bandies the Elders, and mocks at Mess John,
While back in his teeth his own text she flings rarely:
    O, gin my wife wad speak hooly and fairly! 40
        Hooly and fairly, hooly and fairly,
    O, gin my wife wad speak hooly and fairly!

I wish I were single, I wish I were freed;
I wish I were doited, I wish I were dead,
Or she in the mouls, to dement me nae mair, lay!
    What does it 'vail to cry hooly and fairly!
        Hooly and fairly, hooly and fairly,
    Wasting my breath to cry hooly and fairly!

A SCOTTISH SONG:
'THE GOWAN GLITTERS ON THE SWARD'

The gowan glitters on the sward,
    The lavrock's in the sky,
And collie on my plaid keeps ward,
    And time is passing by,
        Oh no! sad and slow
And, lengthened on the ground,
    The shadows of our trysting bush,
It wears so slowly round!

My sheep-bell tinkles frae the west,
    My lambs are bleating near,   10
But still the sound that I lo'e best,
    Alack! I canna' hear.
        Oh no! sad and slow,
The shadow lingers still,
    And like a lanely ghaist I stand
And croon upon the hill.

I hear below the water roar,
    The mill wi' clacking din,
And Lucky scolding frae her door,
    To ca' the bairnies in.   20
        Oh no! sad and slow,
These are na' sounds for me,
    The shadow of our trysting bush,
It creeps sae drearily!

I coft yestreen, frae Chapman Tam,
    A snood of bonny blue,
And promised when our trysting cam',
    To tie it round her brow.
        Oh no! sad and slow,
The mark it winna' pass;   30
    The shadow of that weary thorn,
Is tethered on the grass.

O now I see her on the way,
   She's past the witch's knowe,
She's climbing up the Browny's brae,
   My heart is in a lowe!
     Oh no! 'tis na' so,
'Tis glamrie I have seen;
   The shadow of that hawthorn bush,
Will move na' mair till e'en.   40

My book o' grace I'll try to read,
   Though conn'd wi' little skill,
When collie barks I'll raise my head,
   And find her on the hill;
     Oh no! sad and slow,
The time will ne'er be gane,
   The shadow of the trysting bush,
Is fixed like ony stane.

SONG,
FOR A SCOTTISH AIR:
'O SWIFTLY GLIDES THE BONNY BOAT'

O swiftly glides the bonny boat
   Just parted from the shore,
And, to the fisher's chorus note,
   Soft moves the dipping oar!
His toils are borne with lightsome cheer,
And ever may they speed,
Who feeble age and helpmates dear,
   And tender bairnies feed.

CHORUS

We cast our lines in Largo Bay,
   Our nets are floating wide,   10
Our bonny boat with yielding sway
   Rocks lightly on the tide;

And happy prove our daily lot,
    Upon the summer sea!
And blest on land our kindly cot,
    Where all our treasures be!

The mermaid on her rock may sing,
    The witch may weave her charm,
Nor water-sprite, nor eldrich thing
    The bonny boat can harm.   20
It safely bears its scaly store
    Through many a stormy gale,
While joyful shouts rise from the shore,
    Its homeward prow to hail.

CHORUS

We cast our lines in Largo Bay,
    Our nets are floating wide,
Our bonny boat with yielding sway
    Rocks lightly on the tide;
And happy prove our daily lot,
    Upon the summer sea!   30
And blest on land our kindly cot,
    Where all our treasures be!

SONG,
FOR A SCOTTISH AIR:
'POVERTY PARTS GOOD COMPANY'

When my o'erlay was white as the foam o' the lin,
And siller was chinkin' my pouches within,
When my lambkins were bleatin' on meadow and brae,
As I went to my love in new cleeding sae gay,
        Kind was she, and my friends were free,
        But poverty parts good company.

How swift passed the minutes and hours of delight,
When piper played cheerly, and crusie burned bright,
And linked in my hand was the maiden sae dear,
As she footed the floor in her holy-day gear!   10
      Woe is me; and can it then be,
      That poverty parts sic company?

We met at the fair, and we met at the kirk,
We met i' the sunshine, we met i' the mirk;
And the sound o' her voice, and the blinks o' her een,
The cheerin' and life of my bosom hae been.
      Leaves frae the tree, at Mertimass flee,
      And poverty parts sweet company.

At bridal and infare, I braced me wi' pride,
The bruise I hae won, and a kiss o' the bride;   20
And loud was the laughter good fellows among,
As I uttered my banter or chorused my song;
      Dowie and dree are jestin' and glee,
      When poverty spoils good company.

Wherever I gaed kindly lasses looked sweet,
And mithers and aunties were unco discreet;
While kebbuck and beeker were set on the board;
But now they pass by me, and never a word!
      Sae let it be, for the worldly and slee
      Wi' poverty keep nae company.   30

But the hope of my love is a cure for its smart,
And the spae-wife has tauld me to keep up my heart,
For, wi' my last saxpence, her loof I hae crost,
And the bliss that is fated can never be lost.
      Though cruelly we may ilka day see
      How poverty parts dear company.

SONG:
'FY, LET US A' TO THE WEDDING'
(AN AULD SANG, NEW BUSKIT)

Fy, let us a' to the wedding,
    For they will be lilting there;
For Jock's to be married to Maggy,
    The lass wi' the gowden hair.

And there will be jibing and jeering,
    And glancing of bonny dark een,
Loud laughing and smooth-gabbit speering
    O' questions baith pawky and keen.

And there will be Bessy the beauty,
    Wha raises her cockup sae hie,   10
And giggles at preachings and duty,
    Guid grant that she gang na' ajee!

And there will be auld Geordie Taunner,
    Wha coft a young wife wi' his gowd;
She'll flaunt wi' a silk gown upon her,
    But wow! he looks dowie and cow'd.

And brown Tibby Fouler the Heiress
    Will perk at the tap o' the ha',
Encircled wi' suitors, wha's care is
    To catch up her gloves when they fa', –   20

Repeat a' her jokes as they're cleckit,
    And haver and glower in her face,
When tocherless mays are negleckit, –
    A crying and scandalous case.

And Maysie, wha's clavering aunty
    Wad match her wi' Laurie the Laird,
And learns the young fule to be vaunty,
    But neither to spin nor to caird.

And Andrew, wha's Granny is yearning
    To see him a clerical blade,   30
Was sent to the college for learning,
    And cam' back a coof as he gaed.

And there will be auld Widow Martin,
    That ca's hersel thrity and twa;
And thraw-gabbit Madge wha for certain
    Was jilted by Hab o' the Shaw.

And Elspy the sewster sae genty,
    A pattern of havens and sense,
Will straik on her mittens sae dainty,
    And crack wi' Mess John i' the spence.   40

And Angus, the seer o' fairlies,
    That sits on the stane at his door,
And tells about bogles, and mair lies
    Than tongue ever uttered before.

And there will be Bauldy the boaster,
    Sae ready wi' hands and wi' tongue:
Proud Paty and silly Sam Foster,
    Wha quarrel wi' auld and wi' young.

And Hugh the town-writer, I'm thinking,
    That trades in his lawerly skill,   50
Will egg on the fighting and drinking
    To bring after-grist to his mill:

And Maggy – na, na! we'll be civil,
    And let the wee bridie a-be;
A vilipend tongue is the devil,
    And ne'er was encouraged by me.

Then fy, let us a' to the wedding,
    For they will be lilting there,
Frae mony a far-distant ha'ding,
    The fun and the feasting to share.   60

For they will get sheep's head, and haggis,
        And browst o' the barley-mow;
E'en he that comes latest, and lag is,
        May feast upon dainties enow:

Veal florentines in the oon baken,
        Weel plenished wi' raisins and fat,
Beef, mutton, and chuckies, a' taken
        Het reeking frae spit and frae pat:

And glasses (I trow 'tis na' said ill),
        To drink the young couple good luck,   70
Weel filled wi' a braw beechen ladle
        Frae punch-bowl as big as Dumbuck.

And there will come dancing and daffing,
        And reelin and crossin o' hans,
Till even auld Lucky is laughing,
        As back by the aumry she stans.

Sic bobbing and flinging and whirling,
        While fiddlers are making their din;
And pipes are droning and skirling,
        As loud as the roar o' the lin.   80

They fy, let us a' to the wedding,
        For they will be lilting there,
For Jock's to be married to Maggy,
        The lass wi' the gowden hair.

VERSES WRITTEN IN FEBRUARY, 1827

Like gleam of sunshine on the mountain's side,
Fair, bright and beautiful, while all beside,
Slope, cliff and pinnacle in shadow lie
Beneath the awning of a wintry sky,
Through loop-hole in its cloudy texture beaming
A cataract of light, so softly streaming, –
Shines one blest deed of ruth when war's grim form
O'er a scourged nation guides his passing storm.

    Like verdant islet-spots, that softly peer
Through the dull mist, as morning breezes clear   10
The brooding vapour from the wide-stretched vale,
So in a land where Mammon's cares prevail,
Do frequent deeds of gentle charity
Refresh the moral gazer's mental eye.
    Britain, thou art in arms and commerce graced
With many generous acts, that, fairly traced
On thy long annals, give a lustre far
Exceeding those of wealth or trophied war;
And may we not say truthfully of thee,
Thou art a land of mercy? – May it be!   20

    What forms are those with lean galled sides? In vain
Their laxed and ropy sinews sorely strain
Heaped loads to draw with lash and goad urged on.
They were in other days, but lately gone,
The useful servants, dearly prized, of those
Who to their failing age give no repose, –
Of thankless, heartless owners. Then full oft
Their arched graceful necks so sleek and soft
Beneath a master's stroking hand would rear
Right proudly, as they neighed his well-known voice to hear.   30
But now how changed! – And what marred things are these,
Starved, hooted, scarred, denied or food or ease;
Whose humbled looks their bitter thraldom show,
Familiar with the kick, the pinch, the blow?
Alas! in this sad fellowship are found
The playful kitten and the faithful hound,
The gallant cock that hailed the morning light,
All now hard-fated mates in woeful plight.

Ah no! A land of mercy is a name
Which thou in all thy glory mayest not claim!   40

But yet there dwell in thee the good, the bold,
Who in thy streets, courts, senates bravely hold
Contention with thy wayward cruelty,
And shall subdue it ere this age glide by.
Meantime as they their manly power exert,
'Godspeed ye well!' bursts from each kindly heart.
And they *will* speed, for this foul blot of shame
Must be washed out from Britain's honoured name,
And she among enlightened nations stand,
A brave, a merciful and generous land.   50

SONG,
TO THE SCOTTISH AIR OF 'MY NANNY O'

Wi' lang-legged Tam the bruise I tried,
          Though best o' foot, what wan he o?
The first kiss of the blouzing bride,
          But I the heart of Nanny o.

Like swallow wheeling round her tower,
          Like rock-bird round her cranny o,
Sinsyne I hover near her bower,
          And list and look for Nanny o.

I'm nearly wild, I'm nearly daft,
          Wad fain be douce, but canna' o;   10
There's ne'er a Laird of muir or craft,
          Sa blithe as I wi' Nanny o.

She's sweet, she's young, she's fair, she's good,
          The brightest maid of many o,
Though a' the world our love withstood,
          I'd woo and win my Nanny o.

Her angry mither scalds sa loud,
    And darkly glooms her granny o;
But think they he can e'er be cowed,
    Wha loves and lives for Nanny o?   20

The spae-wife on my loof that blink't
    Is but a leeing ranny o,
For weel kens she my fate is link't
    In spite of a' to Nanny o.

THE MERRY BACHELOR
(FOUNDED ON THE OLD SCOTTISH SONG,
'WILLIE WAS A WANTON WAG')

Willie was a wanton wag,
    The blithest lad that e'er I saw;
Of field and floor he was the brag,
    And carried a' the gree awa'.

And was na' Willie stark and keen,
    When he gaed to the weapon-shaw;
He won the prizes on the green,
    And cheered the feasters in the ha'.

His head was wise, his heart was liel,
    His truth was fair without a flaw;   10
And aye by every honest chiel
    His word was holden as a law.

And was na' Willie still our pride
    When, in his gallant gear arrayed,
He wan the bruise and kissed the bride,
    While pipes the wedding welcome played.

And aye he led the foremost dance,
    Wi' winsome maidens buskit braw,
And gave to each a merry glance
    That stole, a while, her heart awa'.   20

The bride forgot her simple groom,
        And every lass her trysted Joe;
Yet nae man's brow on Will could gloom,
        They liked his rousing blitheness so.

Our good Mess John laughed wi' the laive;
        The dominie for a' his lair
Could scarcely like himsel behave,
        While a' was glee and revel there.

A joyous sight was Willie's face,
        Baith far and near in ilka spot;   30
In ha' received wi' kindly grace,
        And welcomed to the lowly cot.

The carlin left her housewife's wark,
        The bairnies shouted Willie's name;
The colley too would fidge and bark
        And wag his tail when Willie came.

But Willie now has crossed the main,
        And he has been sae lang awa'!
Oh! would he were returned again
        To drive the doufness frae us a!   40

SONG,
A NEW VERSION OF AN OLD SCOTTISH SONG:
'SAW YE JOHNNY COMIN''

'Saw ye Johnny comin'?' quo' she,
'Saw ye Johnny comin'?
Wi' his blue bonnet on his head,
And his doggie runnin'.
Yestreen about the gloamin' time
I chanced to see him comin'
Whistling merrily the tune
That I am a' day hummin',' quo she,
        'I am a' day hummin'.'

'Fee him, faither, fee him,' quo' she,   10
'Fee him, faither, fee him;
A' the wark about the house
Gaes wi' me whan I see him:
A' the wark about the house,
I gang sae lightly through it;
And though ye pay some merks o' geer,
Hoot! ye winna rue it,' quo' she,
      'No; ye winna rue it.'

'What wad I do wi' him, hizzy?
What wad I do wi' him?   20
He's ne'er a sark upon his back,
And I hae nane to gie him.'
'I hae twa sarks into my kist,
And ane o' them I'll gie him;
And for a merk o' mair fee,
O, dinna stand wi' him,' quo' she,
      'Dinna stand wi' him.'

'Weel do I lo'e him,' quo' she,
'Weel do I lo'e him,
The brawest lads about the place   30
Are a' but haverels to him.
O fee him, faither; lang I trow
We've dull and dowie been;
He'll haud the plough, thrash i' the barn,
And crack wi' me at e'en,' quo' she,
      'Crack wi' me at e'en.'

VERSES TO OUR OWN FLOWERY KIRTLED SPRING

Welcome, sweet time of buds and bloom, renewing
The earliest objects of delight, and wooing
The notice of the grateful heart! for then
Long-hidden, beauteous friends are seen again;
From the cleft soil, like babes from cradle peeping,
At the glad light, where soundly they've been sleeping;
Like chickens in their downy coats, just freeing
From the chipped shell, their new-found active being;
Like spotted butterfly, its wings uprearing,
Half from the bursting chrysalis appearing.   10
Sweet season, so bedight, so gay so kind,
Right welcome to the sight and to the mind!

    Now many a 'thing that pretty is' delays
The wanderer's steps beneath the sun's soft rays.
Gay daffodils, bent o'er the watery gleam,
Doubling their flickered image in the stream;
The woody nook where bells of brighter blue
Have clothed the ground in heaven's etherial hue;
The lane's high sloping bank, where pale primrose
With hundreds of its gentle kindred blows;   20
And speckled daisies that on uplands bare
Their round eyes opening, scatter gladness there.
Man looks on nature with a grateful smile,
And thinks of Nature's bounteous Lord the while.

    Now urchins range the brake in joyous bands,
With new-called nosegays in their dimpled hands,
The cottage maid her household task-work cheats
In mead or glen to pick the choicest sweets,
With skilful care reserved for Sunday morn,
Her bosom's simple kerchief to adorn.   30
And even the beldame, as with sober tread,
She takes her sunning in the grassy mead,
Stoops down with eager look and finds, well pleased,
Such herbs, as in a chest or bible squeezed,
In former days were deemed, by folks of sense,
A fragrant wholesome virtue to dispense,
And oft on raftered roof, in bunches strung,
With other winter stores were duly hung.

But not alone in simple scenes like these,
Thy beauteous offspring our soothed senses please;   40
I' the city busy streets, by rich men's doors,
On whose white steps the flower-girl sets her stores,
In wicker basket grouped to lure the sight,
They stop and tempt full many a wistful wight.
Flowers though they be by artful culture bred,
Upon the suburb-seedsman's crowded bed,
By fetid manure cherished, gorgeous, bright,
Like civic madams dressed for festive night, –
Anemones of crimson, purple, yellow,
And tulips streaked with colours rich and mellow,   50
Brown wallflowers and jonquils of golden glare,
In dapper posies tied like shopman's ware,
Yet still they whisper something to the heart,
Which feelings kind and gentle thoughts impart.

Gay sight! that oft a touch of pleasure gives
Even to the saddest, rudest soul that lives –
Gay sight! the passing carman grins thereat,
And sticks a purchased posie in his hat,
And cracks his whip and treads the rugged streets,
With waggish air and jokes with all he meets.   60
The sickly child from nursery window spies
The tempting show, and for a nosegay cries,
Which placed in china mug, by linnet's cage,
Will for a time his listless mind engage.
The dame precise, moves at the flower-girl's cry,
Laying her patch-work or her netting by,
And from the parlour window casts her eye,
Then sends across the way her tiny maid;
And presently on mantlepiece displayed,
Between fair ornaments of chinaware,   70
Small busts and lacquered parrots stationed there,
Tulips, anemones and wallflowers shine,
And strangely with their new compeers combine!
Each visitor with wonder to excite,
Who looks and smiles, and lauds the motley sight.
That even to the prison's wretched thrall,
Those simple gems of nature will recall
What soothes the sadness of his dreary state,

Yon narrow window, through whose iron grate
A squalid countenance is dimly traced,   80
Gazing on flowers in broken pitcher placed
Upon the sooty sill and withering there,
Sad emblems of himself, most piteously declare.

    Of what in gentle lady's curtained room,
On storied stands and gilded tripods bloom,
The richest, rarest flowers of every clime,
Whose learned names suit not my simple rhyme,
I speak not! lovely as they are, we find
They visit more the senses than the mind.
Their nurture comes not from the clouds of heaven,   90
But from a painted watering-pot is given;
And, in return for daily care, with faint
And sickly sweetness hall and chamber taint.
I will not speak of those; we feel and see
They have no kindred, our own Spring! with thee.

    Welcome, sweet season! though with rapid pace
Thy course is run, and we can scarcely grace
Thy joyous coming with a grateful cheer,
Ere loose-leaved flowers and leaflets shrunk and sere,
And flaccid bending stems, sad bodings! tell   100
We soon must bid our fleeting friend farewell.

SCHOOL RHYMES FOR NEGRO CHILDREN

How happy are we in that hour we love,
When shadows grow longer and branches move;
    Blithe urchins then we be!
From the school's low porch with a joyous shout,
We rush and we run and we gambol about,
    So careless, light and free!

And the good child merrily plays his part,
For all is well in his guileless heart,
    The glance of his eye is bright.
We hop and we leap and we toss the ball;   10
Some dance to their shadows upon the wall,
    And spread out their hands with delight.

The parrot that sits on her bough a-swinging,
The bird and the butterfly, light air winging,
    Are serenely more happy, I trow.
Then hey for the meadow, the glade and the grove,
For evening is coming and branches move,
    We'll have merry pastime now.

RHYMES FOR CHANTING

Butterfly, butterfly, speed through the air,
    The ring-bird follows thee fast,
And the monkey looks up with a greedy stare;
    Speed on till the peril be past!

O, wert thou but safe in my garden bower,
    And wouldst thou no further stray,
Thou shouldst feed on the rose and the gilliflower,
    And be my playmate gay.

THE COUNTRY LADY'S REVEILLIE

From early fire wending
The smoke is ascending,
And with the clouds blending,
     Awake, awake!
From green covert creeping
Wild creatures are peeping,
Fy! sloth of dull sleeping
     Forsake, forsake!

The cocks are a-crowing,
The kine are a-lowing,   10
The milk-pail is flowing
     Awake, awake!
The dew-drops are gleaming,
And bright eyes are beaming,
The mist of pale dreaming
     Forsake, forsake!

Now maidens are bracing,
And bodices lacing,
The slender form gracing,
     Awake, awake!   20
On slippered toe stealing,
Thy fair face revealing,
The curtain's dark sheeling
     Forsake, forsake!

SONG:
'BIRD SOARING HIGH'

Bird soaring high, cloud in the sky,
    Where go ye? O where go ye?
Where the smoke from the gipsy's fire is veering,
And our gay little boat, o'er the blue frith steering,
      Will soon bear me.

My thoughts before, on yonder shore,
    Are free as wind, are free as wind,
While this body of mine on its palfrey riding,
Right lazy of pace, or on smooth wave gliding,
      Is far behind.   10

But see I not, yon distant spot?
    O now I see, O now I see!
Where the mist up the distant hill is creeping,
And woods through the morning cloud are peeping,
      There dwelleth she.

Doth gentle sleep her senses steep
    Or does she wake? or does she wake?
Even now perhaps, her dark hair raising,
At her casement she stands, o'er the waters she's gazing,
      All for my sake.   20

Her face is gay as the joyous day,
    And O how sweet! and O how sweet!
Her voice as she utters her modest greeting,
While my heart at the sound is so quickly beating,
      Whene'er we meet!

When time runs on, and weeks are gone,
    Then on that shore, then on that shore,
I'll meet her with all my gay bridesmen bounding,
In light-hearted glee to the minstrel's sounding,
      And part no more.   30

SONG:
'WHAT VOICE IS THIS, THOU EVENING GALE'

What voice is this, thou evening gale!
That mingles with thy rising wail;
And, as it passes, sadly seems
The faint return of youthful dreams?

Though now its strain is wild and drear,
Blithe was it once as skylark's cheer –
Sweet as the nightbird's sweetest song –
Dear is the lisp of infant's tongue.

It was the voice, at whose sweet flow
The heart did beat, and cheek did glow,   10
And lip did smile, and eye did weep,
And motioned love the measure keep.

Oft be thy sound, soft gale of even,
Thus to my wistful fancy given;
And, as I list the swelling strain,
The dead shall seem to live again.

LINES TO AGNES BAILLIE ON HER BIRTHDAY

Dear Agnes, gleamed with joy and dashed with tears,
O'er us have glided almost sixty years
By those whose eyes long closed in death have been,
Two tiny imps, who scarcely stooped to gather
The slender harebell on the purple heather;
No taller than the foxglove's spiky stem,
That dew of morning studs with silvery gem.
Then every butterfly that crossed our view
With joyful shout was greeted as it flew,
And moth and ladybird and beetle bright   10
In sheeny gold were each a wondrous sight.
Then as we paddled barefoot, side by side,
Among the sunny shallows of the Clyde,

Minnows or spotted par with twinkling fin,
Swimming in mazy rings the pool within,
A thrill of gladness through our bosoms sent,
Seen in the power of early wonderment.

      A long perspective to my mind appears,
Looking behind me to that line of years,
And yet through every stage I still can trace   20
Thy visioned form, from childhood's morning grace
To woman's early bloom, changing how soon!
To the expressive glow of woman's noon;
And now to what thou art, in comely age,
Active and ardent. Let what will engage
Thy present moment, whether hopeful seeds
In garden-plat thou sow, or noxious weeds
From the fair flower remove, or ancient lore
In chronicle or legend rare explore,
Or on the parlour hearth with kitten play,   30
Stroking its tabby sides, or take thy way
To gain with hasty steps some cottage door,
On helpful errand to the neighbouring poor,
Active and ardent, to my fancy's eye,
Thou still art young in spite of time gone by.
Though oft of patience brief and temper keen
Well may it please me, in life's latter scene,
To think what now thou art and long to me hast been.

      'Twas thou who wooedst me first to look
Upon the page of printed book,   40
That thing by me abhorred, and with address
Didst win me from my thoughtless idleness,
When all too old become with bootless haste
In fitful sports the precious time to waste.
Thy love of tale and story was the stroke
At which my dormant fancy first awoke,
And ghosts and witches in my busy brain
Arose in sombre show, a motley train.
This new-found path attempting proud was I,
Lurking approval on thy face to spy,   50
Or hear thee say, as grew thy roused attention,
'What! Is this story all thine own invention?'

Then, as advancing through this mortal span,
Our intercourse with the mixed world began,
Thy fairer face and sprightlier courtesy,
(A truth that from my youthful vanity
Lay not concealed) did for the sisters twain,
Where'er we went, the greater favour gain;
While, but for thee, vexed with its tossing tide,
I from the busy world had shrunk aside.   60
And now in later years, with better grace
Thou helpest me still to hold a welcome place
With those whom nearer neighbourhood have made
The friendlier cheerers of our evening shade.

With thee my humours, whether grave or gay,
Or gracious or untoward, have their way.
Silent if dull – O precious privilege!
I sit by thee; or if, culled from the page
Of some huge, ponderous tome which, but thyself,
None e'er had taken from its dusty shelf,   70
Thou read me curious passages to speed
The winter night, I take but little heed
And thankless say, 'I cannot listen now,'
'Tis no offence; albeit, much do I owe
To these, thy nightly offerings of affection,
Drawn from thy ready talent for selection;
For still it seemed in thee a natural gift
The lettered grain from lettered chaff to sift.

By daily use and circumstance endeared,
Things are of value now that once appeared   80
Of no account, and without notice past,
Which o'er dull life a simple cheering cast;
To hear thy morning steps the stair descending,
Thy voice with other sounds domestic blending;
After each stated nightly absence, met
To see thee by the morning table set,
Pouring from smoky spout the amber stream
Which sends from saucered cup its fragrant steam;
To see thee cheerly on the threshold stand,
On summer morn, with trowel in thy hand   90
For garden-work prepared; in winter's gloom

From thy cold noonday walk to see thee come,
In furry garment lapped, with spattered feet
And by the fire resume thy wonted seat;
Aye even o'er things like these, soothed age has thrown
A sober charm they did not always own.
As winter-hoarfrost makes minutest spray
Of bush or hedge-weed sparkle to the day,
In magnitude and beauty, which bereaved
Of such investment, eye had ne'er perceived.   100

     The change of good and evil to abide,
As partners linked, long have we side by side
Our earthly journey held, and who can say
How near the end of our united way?
By nature's course not distant; sad and 'reft
Will she remain – the lonely pilgrim left.
If thou art taken first, who can to me
Like sister, friend and home-companion be?
Or who, of wonted daily kindness shorn,
Shall feel such loss, or mourn as I shall mourn?   110
And if I should be fated first to leave
This earthly house, though gentle friends may grieve,
And he above them all, so truly proved
A friend and brother, long and justly loved,
There is no living wight, of woman born,
Who then shall mourn for me as thou wilt mourn.

     Thou ardent, liberal spirit! quickly feeling
The touch of sympathy and kindly dealing
With sorrow or distress, forever sharing
The unhoarded mite, nor for tomorrow caring –   120
Accept, dear Agnes, on thy natal day,
An unadorned but not a careless lay.
Nor think this tribute to thy virtues paid
From tardy love proceeds, though long delayed.
Word of affection, howso'er expressed,
The latest spoken still are deemed the best:
Few are the measured rhymes I now may write;
These are, perhaps, the last I shall indite.

SELECT VERSES FROM THE 147th PSALM

Praise ye the Lord with cheerful voice,
In swelling strains His praises sing,
It makes the grateful heart rejoice,
It is a blest and pleasant thing.

He who the broken heart doth brace,
And bindeth up the wounded frame,
Numbers the host through heaven's vast space,
And gives to every star its name.

With fleecy clouds He clothes the sky,
He stores the moistened earth with good,   10
From Him the ravens when they cry,
And savage beasts receive their food.

He sends afar His high behests,
Which sea and land with blessings fill;
Swift flies His word, no power arrests
The course of His almighty will.

HYMN:
'MY SOUL! AND DOST THOU FAINTLY SHRINK'

My soul! And dost thou faintly shrink,
Thus trembling on an awful brink?
Or rough, or smooth, but one step more,
And thy long pilgrimage is o'er.
Thy pilgrim's cloak that clipped thee round,
Like a seared leaf, dropped on the ground,
A base and mouldering thing shall lie,
Its form and uses all gone by.
Behind thee, closing darkness all
Shall cover, like a midnight pall;   10
Before thee – No! I may not dare
To think, or fancy, what lies there. –

Doth the unbodied spirit take its flight,
Unto its destined, distant, sphere of light,
Upon the buoyant wings of morn,
　　　All conscious of its glory borne:
　　　Or with an instant transit, make
　　　The awful change, and then awake,
　　　As from a slumber, sound and deep,
　　　Awakes an infant from its sleep,　　　　　　　20
　　　With limbs refreshed and vigour new
　　　A gradual progress to pursue;
Allied to infancy, with earthly charms,
Once fondled in an elder brother's arms,
Who said to men, by worldly passions driven,
'Lo! such as these possess the realms of heaven.'

　　　Or shall it powerful, and at once
　　　Start up as from a gloomy trance,
　　　With sudden, glorious light astounded,
By the blest brotherhood of saints surrounded,　　　30
Where those, who have been loved and lost, appear
With kindred looks of greeting and of cheer?

　　　Away, ye pictured thoughts that pass
　　　Like figures on a magic glass,
　　　Or fitful light with arrowy rays
　　　That on the northern welkin plays!
　　　A steady gleam that will not flit,
　　　Come from the words of Holy Writ.
　　　'Eye hath not seen, and ear hath never heard,
Nor heart conceived the things by God prepared,　　　40
For those who love Him.' – O such love impart,
　　　Repentant, fervent, and adoring,
　　　From every taint of sin restoring,
My Father and my God! to this poor heart!

RECOLLECTIONS OF A DEAR AND STEADY FRIEND

When life's long pilgrimage draws to a close,
A backward glance the weary traveller throws
On many a league traversed, and views the road,
Distant and near, in long perspective trod
By him and by companions on his way,
Who still hold onward, whether grave or gay,
Through gloom and gleam; a checkered path, I ween,
Where forms within the memory's ken are seen,
Forms faint or vivid, varying oft, that seem
Like moving objects in a seried dream: 10
Till one right clearly on the mind impressed
Bears for a time his thoughts from all the rest,
And, undisturbed upon his peaceful station,
His busy mind enjoys its mournful occupation.

       There she appears, as when in virgin grace
I first beheld her laughing, lovely face,
Intelligent withal, in which combined
Seemed every hopeful quality of mind,
Solace, and cheer, and counsel, to impart,
All that should win and hold a manly, generous heart.   20

       I see her mated with a moody lord,
Whose fame she prized, whose genius she adored.
There by his side she stands, pale, grave, and sad;
The brightness of her greeting smile is fled.
Like some fair flower ta'en from its genial mould
To deck a garden border, loose and cold,
Its former kindred fences all destroyed,
Shook by the breeze and by the rake annoyed,
She seemed, alas! – I looked and looked again,
Tracing the sweet but altered face in vain.   30

       I see her next in agony of soul:
Her surcharged feelings broken from all control:
The hand upon her forehead closely pressed,
The trembling frame and quivering lips expressed,
Though scarcely audible the feeble mutter,
Far more than full articulate sounds could utter.

I see her when by pure religion taught
Her heart is lightened of its heavy fraught.
Her canopy of murky clouds hath passed,
In air dissolved, and sunshine gleams at last.   40
Her heart, with Christian charity imbued,
Hath every hard vindictive thought subdued.
Oh, then how fair a sight it was to trace
That blessed state upon her placid face!
And yet, when weary of the gossip sound
From morning visitors convening round,
She would at times unusual silence hold,
Some, ah how erringly! believed her stiff and cold.

I see her from the world retired caressing
Her infant daughter, her assured blessing;   50
Teaching the comely creature, in despite
Of forward freaks, to feel and act aright;
Well suiting to her task her voice and look
With fondling playfulness or grave rebuke.
Now, with expression changed, but sweet, she cheers
Her widowed father's weary weight of years.
How slily does her gentle hint recall
Some half-forgotten tale of cot or hall,
To raise his hearty laugh, as by the fire
In easy chair he sits! old tales that never tire.   60

To early friends her love was firm and fast;
Beneath her roof they gathered oft and cast
A faint reflected gleam of days gone by,
And kindly smiled on them her soft blue eye.
One dearly prized may special notice claim,
Mary Montgomery! nobly sounding name,
And worthy she to bear it. Oft would come
Their youthful kindred; to an easy home,
Where they might still their fairy gambols hold,
Nor in her presence fear to be too bold.   70
Though tired and languid, laid awhile to rest,
Around her still the active urchins pressed,
Would o'er the tumbled covering strive and wrestle,
And e'en at times behind her snugly nestle.
At hide and seek where did they lurk and crouch?

Ay, where forsooth but in my lady's couch!
Mock frowns from her but small impression made,
They gambolled on, and would not be afraid.

Books were her solace, whether grave or gay,
But most she loved the poet's plaintive lay;   80
And e'en at times with knit considerate brow
Would with her pen a native talent show.
When fancy, linked with feelings kind and dear,
Was found in lines that did not please the ear,
O then, with what a countenance she met
Her certain fate, by critics sore beset!
She met it all with simple kindly air,
The first to own and then the fault repair.

Mistress at length of wealth and large domain,
Behold her now a modest state maintain,   90
With generous heart and liberal hand bestowing, –
A spring of friendly kindness, ever flowing.
She did with such a gentle ease relieve,
From her it was a pleasure to receive.
With consideration of a friend,
All was arranged to serve a useful end,
And no humiliation could ensue
To make the wounded heart her bounty rue.
Nay, rather its condition seemed to rise,
Knit to her then as if by kindred ties.   100
For worth distressed there was in sooth no need
In earnest piteous words with her to plead,
Nor feel, because of some slight boons obtained,
But recently perhaps, shy and restrained:
Her cheerful eye gave answer short and plain,
'Think not of that, but come and come again.'

The humming of her school, its morning sound,
With all her youthful scholars gathered round;
Their shout, when issuing forth at midday hour,
Each active lad exerting all his power   110
To do the sturdy labour of a man,
As through the groups quick emulation ran,
Was music to her ear; warm thrilled her blood;

She felt she was promoting public good.
And have I seen her proud or heard her boast?
Yes, once I did; when, counting use and cost,
She gravely added, that the boys thus trained,
Employment afterwards more surely gained
From farmer, or from village artisan,
Who trusted each would prove a steady man.   120
In truth, her school had in its humble station
Acquired an honest fame and reputation.

      I've seen when in a daughter's happy lot
Her own was brightened, woes and cares forgot.
While with a roguish grandchild few could quell,
A sturdy imp that loved his grandame well,
She lowly sate upon the carpet playing,
The former frolics of her youth betraying, –
A pleasing sight, that led to deep reflection;
To pain and pleasure linked in close connection.   130

      And now within her chamber-walls confined
She sadly dwells and strives to be resigned,
Her span of life, yet short, though rough the past,
May still through further years of languor last,
Or health to other years may yet be given
To do her Master's will – the will of heaven.
But should her lot be pain and sickness still,
She hath her task of duty to fulfill –
Her task of love, cheered by her noble trust,
The Christian's lofty faith, that from the dust   140
Lifts up the Christian's head, gleams in his eye,
Bracing his wasted strength to live or die.
Ay, 'tis a noble faith, not fenced and bound
By orthodoxy's narrow plot of ground,
The Bible, not the Church, directs her way,
Nor does he through entangled labyrinths stray.
Before her stands a prospect fair and wide,
To endless distance stretched on either side;
A generous Saviour, beckoning us to come
Where mercy has prepared our peaceful home;   150
Where God, His God, supreme all powers above,
Receives us in the realms of sanctity and love.

If late or early from her house of clay,
The lease expired, her soul be turned away,
What boots it? ready for her Master's call,
Death's gloomy pass no longer can appal.
The covering o'er a pallid face is thrown,
The coffin closed, and all the rest unknown –
'No, not unknown,' a conscious spirit cries,
Stirring within us quickly; we shall rise   160
To nobler being waked; heaven's glorious show,
The varied wonders of the earth below,
And He who spake as never man did speak,
All tell of future happiness to break
On the departed just, whilst Nature's voice
Of many tones doth in that mighty sound rejoice.

But in what order we shall leave this scene,
Where all our joys, affections, cares have been,
Ah! who can say? the young and strong may stand
Close to the hidden confines of that land   170
From which no traveller returns again,
Whose sights and sounds in mystery remain:
But there full surely do the aged wait
An hourly summons to the unknown state.
Report perhaps of my decease may find
Her on a weary couch of pain reclined,
And some dear silent watcher then may see
Her soft eye glistening with a tear for me –
But cease we here – o'er fancy's sight is thrown
A closing veil – my visioned thoughts are gone.   180

THE WEARY PUND O' TOW

A young gudewife is in my house,
            And thrifty means to be,
But aye she's runnin' to the town,
            Some ferlie there to see.
The weary pund, the weary pund, the weary pund o' tow,
I soothly think, ere it be spun, I'll wear a lyart pow.

And when she sets her to her wheel
    To draw her threads wi' care,
In comes the chapman wi' his gear,
    And she can spin nae mair.   10
The weary pund, the weary pund, the weary pund o' tow,
I soothly think, ere it be spun, I'll wear a lyart pow.

And she, like ony merry may,
    At fairs maun still be seen,
At kirkyard preachings near the tent,
    At dances on the green.
The weary pund, the weary pund, the weary pund o' tow,
I soothly think, ere it be spun, I'll wear a lyart pow.

Her dainty ear a fiddle charms,
    A bagpipe's her delight,   20
But for the crooning o' her wheel
    She disna care a mite.
The weary pund, the weary pund, the weary pund o' tow,
I soothly think, ere it be spun, I'll wear a lyart pow.

You spake, my Kate, of snaw-white webs,
    Made o' your linkum twine,
But ah! I fear our bonny burn
    Will ne'er lave web o' thine.
The weary pund, the weary pund, the weary pund o' tow,
I soothly think, ere it be spun, I'll wear a lyart pow.   30

Nay, smile again, my winsome mate,
    Sic jeering means nae ill,
Should I gae sarkless to my grave,
    I'll lo'e and bless thee still.
The weary pund, the weary pund, the weary pund o' tow,
I soothly think, ere it be spun, I'll wear a lyart pow.

TAM O' THE LIN

Tam o' the Lin was fu' o' pride,
And his weapon he girt to his valorous side,
A scabbard o' leather wi' deil-haet within, –
'Attack me wha daur!' quo' Tam o' the Lin.

Tam o' the Lin he bought a mear
She cost him five shilling, she was na' dear,
Her back stuck up and her sides fell in, –
'A fiery yaud,' quo' Tam o' the Lin.

Tam o' the Lin he courted a may,
She stared at him sourly and said him nay,   10
But he stroked down his jerkin and cock'd up his chin, –
'She aims at a laird then,' quo' Tam o' the Lin.

Tam o' the Lin he gaed to the fair,
Yet he look'd wi' disdain on the chapman's ware,
Then chuck'd out a saxpence, the saxpence was tin, –
'There's coin for the fiddlers,' quo' Tam o' the Lin.

Tam o' the Lin wad show his lare,
And he scann'd o'er the book wi' a wiselike stare,
He muttered confusedly but didna begin, –
'This is Dominie's business,' quo' Tam o' the Lin.   20

Tam o' the Lin had a cow wi' ae horn,
That liket to feed on his neighbour's corn,
The stanes he threw at her fell short o' her skin, –
'She's a lucky old reiver,' quo' Tam o' the Lin.

Tam o' the Lin he married a wife,
And she was the torment, the plague o' his life;
She lays sae about her, and makes sic a din, –
'She frightens the bailie,' quo' Tam o' the Lin.

Tam o' the Lin grew dowie and douce,
And he sat on a stane at the end o' his house: 30
What ails thee, auld chield? he looks haggard and thin, –
'I'm no vera cheery,' quo' Tam o' the Lin.

Tam o' the Lin lay down to die,
And his friends whisper'd softly and woefully,
We'll buy you some masses to scour away sin, –
'And drink at my latewake,' quo' Tam o' the Lin.

NEW WORDS TO THE OLD SCOTCH AIR
OF 'THE WEE PICKLE TOW'

A lively young lass had a wee pickle tow,
And she thought to try the spinning o't;
She sat by the fire and her rock took a low,
And that was an ill beginning o't.
Loud and shrill was the cry that she utter'd I ween;
The sudden mischanter brought tears to her een;
Her face it was fair, but her temper was keen;
O dole for the ill beginning o't!

She stamp'd on the floor and her twa hands she wrung,
Her bonnie sweet mon' she crooket o!   10
And fell was the outbreak o' words fra her tongue;
Like one sair demented she looket o!
'Foul fa' the inventor o' rock and o' reel!
I hope, guid forgie me, he's now wi' the deil,
He brought us mair trouble than help, wot I weel,
O dole for the ill beginning o't!'

And now when they're spinning and kemping awa',
They'll talk o' my rock, and the burning o't,
While Tibbie, and Mysie, and Maggie and a'
Into some silly joke will be turning it;   20
They'll say I was doited, they'll say I was fou',
They'll say I was dowie, and Robin untrue,
They'll say in the fire some luve-pouther I threw,
And that made the ill beginning o't!

O curst be the day and unchancy the hour,
When I sat me adown to the spinning o't!
Then some evil spirit or warlock had pow'r,
And made sic an ill beginning o't:
May Spunkie my feet to the boggie betray,
The lunzie folk steal my new kirtle away,   30
And Robin forsake me for douce Effie Gray,
The next time I try the spinning o't!

Notes on the poems

A Winter Day

'A Winter Day' and 'A Summer Day' (*Poems*, 1790) are blank verse poems which are aligned with as well as subversive of the tradition of the pastoral. In particular, Baillie's two poems on the seasons are an ironic response to Pope's *Four Pastorals* (1709) and carry echoes of *The Seasons* (1726-1730) by the Scottish poet, James Thomson. Baillie can be seen to have developed this tradition; for example, she eschews neo-classical musing on winter and summer, and uses less elevated language than her well-known predecessors. By drawing on her detailed observation of the lives of the country people whom she knew as a child in her father's parishes at Bothwell and Hamilton and later on her mother's family estate at Long Calderwood in the Scottish Lowlands, she represents the joys and sorrows of individuals in rural settings. Thus Baillie's poems cannot be taken as patronage of those in a class lower than herself; for, as she herself later noted, she had taken part in their lives: 'Traits in human nature whether in books or in real life have always had most power in arresting my attention and keeping place in my recollection. This has often made me a watcher of children at play or under any excitement, and/or frequenter in early life of the habitations of labouring and country people which happily for me I had many opportunities of doing' (*Recollections Written at the Request of Miss Berry*, 1831). The origins of Baillie's evocation of rural scenes can be seen in some of her letters; for example, she describes her enjoyment of winter sports when she was a child: 'At first . . . it was the time for sliding on the ice, scampering over the snow or striving against wind & rain with my frock over my head, a thing I delighted in . . .' (letter to Sir Walter Scott, 27 March 1826, MS. 3902, f. 157, National Library of Scotland). She also told Sir George Beaumont, 'Some 50 years ago, I slid upon the ice the whole morning and wondered that people called it cold' (letter to Sir George Beaumont, 22 December 1824, *Notes and Queries*, vol. 174 (1938), pp. 146-7).

7   *hind*   often defined as a married skilled farmworker who occupies a farm-cottage and has certain perquisites in addition to wages; a cottar. But Baillie herself explained in *Fugitive Verses* (1840) that '*Hind* does not perfectly express the condition of the person here intended, who is somewhat above a common labourer – the tenant of a very small farm, which he cultivates with his own hands; a few cows, perhaps a horse, and some six or seven sheep, being all the wealth he possessed. A class of men very common in the west of Scotland, ere political economy was thought of.' For a complete reprinting of her later variant version of 'A Winter's Day' (*Fugitive Verses*, 1840), see my anthology,

Women Romantic Poets, 1785-1832, Everyman/Dent, 1992; new edn, 1994, pp. 43-52.

30   *corn*   oats or other grain.

36   *flail*   hand-threshing instrument.

38   *cot*   cottage.

68   *grumly*   sullen. Cf. *Fugitive Verses* (1840):

> The morning vapour rests upon the heights,
> Lurid and red, while growing gradual shades
> Of pale and sickly light spread o'er the sky.   (ll. 69-71).

68-84   Cf. James Thomson, 'Winter' (1726), ll. 112-19 for a more elevated personification of winter.

77   *crusted*   layered with snow or frost.

79   *slide*   a track on ice for sliding.

103   *husbandman*   a man who held land in return for rent.

117   *laborious*   industrious.

124   *wheel*   spinning-wheel.

125   *Rough grating cards*   The wool-card's grating (*Fugitive Verses*, 1840).

128   *thunder*   gun-shot.

141   *partlets*   hens.

148   *fowler*   hunter (of wildfowl).

152   *kine*   cows.

170-81   Cf. William Wordsworth, *The Prelude*, Book I, ll. 425-46.

170   *knotted shoes*   'studded shoes' (*Fugitive Verses*, 1840).

188-235   Cf. George Crabbe, *The Village* (1783) for another view of contemporary social treatment of the poor.

243   *without a glass*   without alcohol. Baillie omits this line in her revised version, 'A Winter's Day' (1840).

250   *horse's head*   that the horse would win a race.

256   In her later revised edition, Baillie inserted here the old Scots marriage custom of holding a foot-race from the church to the wedding reception:

> Or won the bridal race with savoury brose
> And first kiss of the bonny bride, though all
> The fleetest youngsters of the parish strove
> In rivalry against him.   (*Fugitive Verses*, 1840).

278-9 *With peaceful . . . pleasure* The peace of rural life is contrasted favourably with the unsteady pace of town life. Baillie in her second version, *A Winter's Day* (1840), inserted the following additional lines 279-99:

> Then all break up, and, by their several paths,
> Hie homeward, with the evening pastime cheered
> Far more, belike, than those who issue forth
> From city theatre's gay scenic show,
> Or crowded ballroom's splendid moving maze.
> But where the song and story, joke and gibe,
> So lately circled, what a solemn change
> In little time takes place!
> The sound of psalms, by mingled voices raised
> Of young and old, upon the night air borne,
> Haply to some benighted traveller,
> Or the late parted neighbours on their way,
> A pleasing notice gives, that those whose sires
> In former days on the bare mountain's side,
> In deserts, heaths, and caverns, praise and prayer,
> At peril of their lives, in their own form
> Of covenanted worship offered up,
> In peace and safety in their own quiet home
> Are (as in quaint and modest phrase is termed)
> Engaged now in *evening exercise.*

Baillie added the following note: 'In the first edition of 'A Winter's Day', nothing regarding family worship was mentioned; a great omission for which I justly take shame to myself. "The evening exercise", as it was called, prevailed in every house over the simple country parts of the west of Scotland, and I have often heard the sound of it passing through the twilight air, in returning from a late walk.'

A Summer Day

This poem, in language and mood, contrasts directly with the previous poem. In 'A Summer Day', the characterization of farm labourers and smallholding farmers is extended to include young men and women who engage in ribaldry and flirtation during haymaking.

12 *wandering fire* phosphorescent light (will-o'-the-wisp).

14 *benighted* overtaken by night.

47 *fain* gladly.

74 *swain* rustic young man.

81   *doublet all unbraced*   a loose garment without a belt.

82   *sideling bend*   moving sideways.

84   *mead*   meadow.

98   *complaisance*   politeness.

100   *rick*   haystack.

101   *parish toast*   a woman who is much feted by men in the parish.

114-28   Cf. George Crabbe, *The Village* (1783), ll. 41-8.

123   *gusty*   tasty.

139   *nice*   fastidious.

153   *mealy*   the colour of oatmeal.

201   *cumbrous*   cumbersome.

223-4   *And straddling . . . sand*   the boys pretend that the old man's stick is a horse that they ride.

237-40   *The silken clad . . . not so*   Baillie compares unfavourably the manners of the high-born with those of the country folk who are respectful to the old man.

269   *spindle*   pin in spinning-wheel used for twisting and winding the thread;   *distaff*   cleft stick for holding wool or flax wound for spinning by hand.

278   *sweepy*   extending in a continuous slope.

280   *rifted*   with valleys.

293   *copse*   undergrowth.

A Reverie

In this narrative poem in heroic couplets (*Poems*, 1790), an impersonal narrator creates a setting in which the anti-hero, Robin, 'mutters' an interior monologue about his fantasies in anticipation of marriage. This poem evolves from and also treats with ironic humour the tradition of the pastoral which is typified by poems such as Pope's 'Ode on Solitude' (1717). Baillie's language is more specific, her characters and setting more down-to-earth, and her humour less artificial.

Title   'Reverie' in Scots English means 'nonsense or foolish talk' and in standard English refers to 'abstract musing'. This ambiguity in the title implies that daydreams about marriage might turn out to be nonsensical in the light of reality.

4   *parson*   any clergyman.

9   *unbraced*   unbelted.

13   *erst*   formerly.

17   *hosen*   stockings.

20   *rook*   a crow;   *daw*   a jackdaw.

21   *rampy*   wild, unrestrained.

33   *tightest*   most shapely.

45-50   *Ah! happy . . . field.*   An ironic reference to the opening lines of Pope's 'Ode on Solitude' (1717) as well as to his *Windsor Forest* (1713), ll. 235-40.

49   *wattled pales*   intertwined stakes in fencing.

60   *hind*   [see note for 'A Winter Day'].

62   *dower*   dowry.

79   *cheat*   deceit.

84   *wain*   a waggon.

89   *scours*   rushes / runs at a quick pace.

A Disappointment

This comic poem in heroic couplets (*Poems*, 1790) also sends up the tradition of pastoral poetry in both subject matter and its treatment. Baillie, in her representation of a rejected suitor who becomes a comic figure in the face of his moneygrubbing sweetheart and his victorious rival, satirizes social conventions of courtship and marriage in an ironic manner that is comparable with the style of Burns's narrative poem, 'Tam o' Shanter' that was published in the very same year. 'A Disappointment' is similar in form to 'A Reverie' in that the story is introduced through a third-person narrator whose setting of the scene is succeeded by an interior monologue from the anti-hero, William.

12   *clouted shoon*   mended shoes.

15   *reft*   deprived.

21   *niggard*   miserly dotard, a feeble-minded old person.

25   *meed*   reward.

27   *banns*   notice in church of intended marriage, read on three Sundays to give opportunity of objection.

34   *fairing*   present bought at a fair.

34 *lots* pieces of land allotted to a particular tenant. Metaphorically, chance or fate in relation to his choice of partner.

39 *tripped* danced.

40 *ween* surmise; guess; imagine.

43 *swain* rustic lover.

50 *bonnet* men's round brimless Scotch cap.

56 *fiend* devil.

60 *hedgers* makers of hedges; *mattocks* agricultural tools in the shape of picks.

69 *wag* a facetious fellow.

71 *toasts* women honoured in toasts by drinking men; *belles* reigning beauties.

72 *matrons* married women, especially those of dignity and sobriety.

78 *hindmost* furthest behind.

A Lamentation

This poem, also in heroic couplets (*Poems*, 1790), is similar in form to 'A Reverie' and 'A Disappointment', in that the scene is set in a graveyard by an impersonal narrator and is followed by an interior monologue from the anti-hero, Basil, who has lost his beloved in death. In this narrative, Baillie satirizes the 'Graveyard School' of poets, thus named because of their poems on death and human mortality (see, for example, Thomas Grey, 'Elegy in a Country Churchyard', 1751). Baillie eschews the Christian moralizing that is a dominant note of the 'Graveyard School'. Instead she mocks the broken-hearted lover by describing him running home in ridiculous haste when his 'plaint' has been interrupted by the tolling of the church-bell.

4 *motey* flecked with specks of dust.

37 *lightsome* cheering; enlivening; pleasant.

85 *pile* a large building or edifice.

An Address to the Muses

This lyric (*Poems*, 1790) is traditional in its attribution of the difficulties of the aspiring poet to a lack in the nine Muses of Greek mythology. In a series of sestets, Baillie conventionally evokes the spirits of the Muses until she bemoans her own lack of inspiration by them for her own poetry (stanzas 12-14 and 24-5).

1   *tuneful Sisters*   In Greek mythology, the Muses are said to be the nine daughters of Zeus and Mnemosyne, who presided over Mount Parnassus, the seat of the arts.

36   *votaries*   devoted adherents.

38   *fane*   temple.

132-7   *From him . . . to tell.*   In these lines, Baillie anticipates a theme of her 'Introductory Discourse', *A Series of Plays*, 1798, facsimile edn, 1990, p. 42: 'those strong passions that, with small assistance from outward circumstances, work their way in the heart, till they become the tyrannical masters of it, carry on a similar operation in the breast of the monarch, and the man of low degree.' Baillie implies that everyone potentially has the feelings of a poet, but that only the 'bard' has the responsibility for creating poems as art.

147   *with simple words to tell my tale*   Baillie suggests here that she herself is not inspired by the Muses to write elevated poetry, but that, nevertheless, she will create her own poems in plain language.

The Storm-Beat Maid (Somewhat After the Style of Our Old English Ballads)

This ballad (*Poems*, 1790) in conventional quatrains tells the story of a young girl who hysterically braves a storm to seek out her beloved who intends to marry a richer woman than she is. When she reaches her lover's castle he feels so guilt-stricken at the sight of her demented state that he determines never to forsake her again. Interest in poems modelled on oral ballads formed part of that literary revival of earlier styles that was engendered by publications such as Thomas Percy's *Reliques of Ancient Poetry* (1756). Baillie's 'The Storm-Beat Maid' anticipates the literary ballads of William Wordsworth and S. T. Coleridge, and subsequently, John Keats, all of whom made the 'lyrical ballad' a popular genre in the Romantic period.

1   *shrouded*   this past participle suggests the death-like nature of the maid's journey.

51   *buskins*   half-boots.

55   *dight*   clothed, arrayed.

74   *mantle*   loose sleeveless cloak.

91   *sheeted torn*   pale.

101   *ungirt*   unbelted or uncovered.

114   *unmeet*   unsuited.

117   *weeds*   deep mourning worn by a widow.

147   *dizened*   bedizened, that is, decked out gaudily.

An Address to the Night

In these four linked poems (*Poems*, 1790) under the parallel subtitles – 'A Fearful Mind', 'A Discontented Mind', 'A Sorrowful Mind' and 'A Joyful Mind' – Baillie attempts to encapsulate, in rhyming couplets, four distinctive psychological states of mind which might influence perception. Jonathan Wordsworth writes about these four poems, 'The 1790 studies are an attempt to portray mood without personality – temperament, with no narrative implication' ('Introduction', *Poems*, 1790, facsimile edn., p. 2). Baillie later published what she termed in a letter to Sir Walter Scott (15 August 1811, National Library of Scotland, MS. 3881, f. 15) her 'Tragedy on Fear' (*The Dream*, in *Plays of the Passions*, Vol. 3, 1812).

A Discontented Mind

19   *coveys*   broods of partridges.

A Sorrowful Mind

14   *kine*   cows.

27   *cumbrous*   cumbersome, clumsy.

A Joyful Mind

16   *dight*   clothed, arrayed.

71   *winged griffith*   a Scots alternative for 'griffin', a creature of fable with eagle's head and lion's body.

A Mother to Her Waking Infant

This lyric (*Poems*, 1790), in rhyming sestets (with one octet), reflects Scottish enlightened interest in and observation of human behaviour from infancy; and this poems shows how Baillie herself had made precise observations of, for example, a baby's inability to differentiate between joy and sorrow. Baillie's Hunter uncles, and her brother, Matthew, in the medical profession, contributed to the development of Baillie's interest in psychosocial behaviour, an interest which is reflected in the subjects of both her lyric poetry and her drama. In relation to form and language, Jerome McGann has demonstrated how 'A Mother to Her Waking Infant' reflects the rhetorical conventions of the poetry of sensibility (*The Poetics of Sensibility: A Revolution in Literary Style*, 1996, p. 70).

A Child to His Sick Grandfather

This lyric (*Poems*, 1790) is also in rhyming sestets and falls partly into the category of what McGann terms 'the traditions of sensibility and sentiment' (*The Poetics of Sensibility*, p. 1). The first-person speaker, who is represented as a naive child, reveals his inner sentiments about a loved relative.

47-8   The child's grandfather has probably died.

The Kitten

This poem, which was first published in the *Edinburgh Annual Register* (1808), describes, in rhyming tetrameters, a kitten at play. Baillie wrote to Sir Walter Scott in reference to this poem: 'It is a thing I wrote some years ago from a little circumstance. Hearing my sister [Agnes] as she stroked her kitten one day by the fireside say, "Your claws are like the prickles of a rosebud, kitty", I was pleased with the fancy, and took it up' (letter to Sir Walter Scott, 4 November 1809, National Library of Scotland MS. 3878, f. 189).

1   *droll*   amusing.

2   *rustic*   countryman.

8   *faggot*   bundle of sticks or twigs bound together as fuel.

15   *spindle*   pin in spinning-wheel used for twisting and winding the thread.

21   *bootless*   unavailing.

24   *jetty*   jet-black.

30   *kirtle*   woman's gown or outer petticoat.

35   *the jet*   the thrust.

38   *somerset*   somersault.

43   *featest . . . bedight*   the most dextrous tumbler arranged for the stage.

44   *wight*   person.

Song: 'O Welcome Bat and Owlet Gray', Written for a Welsh Air, Called 'The Pursuit of Love'

This poem was sent to George Thomson in February 1804, after he had asked her for contributions for one of his projected anthologies (BL Add. MS. 35263, f. 221). The poem was first printed in his *A Select Collection of Original Welsh*

Airs, 1 (1809), p. 8, for which Joseph Haydn (1732-1809) composed the musical accompaniment for pianoforte or harp, violin and violincello.

1   Thomson asked Baillie to delete 'moth' and substitute 'every drowsy fly' but she refused (BL Add. MS. 35263, f. 304).

12   *stilly*   quiet.

The Black Cock: Written for a Welsh Air, Called 'The Note of the Black Cock'

This poem was also one of the songs that Baillie sent to George Thomson in November 1804 (BL Add MS. 35263, f. 247) as a response to his request for poems to be set to Welsh airs. It was first published in his *A Select Collection of Original Welsh Airs*, 1 (1809), p. 24.

Title: The 'blackcock' is a type of grouse (*Lyrurus tetrix*). The 'Blackcock is easily distinguished by glossy *blue-black* plumage with *lyre-shaped tail*, conspicuous *white under tail coverts and white wing-bar*. . . . Both sexes have scarlet wattle above eye'. Its habitat is 'Near trees bordering moors, marshy ground with rushes and scattered trees, peat-mosses, rocky heather-covered hills, plantations etc.' in the North and West of Great Britain (Roger Peterson, Guy Mountfort and P. A. D. Hollom, *A Field Guide to the Birds of Britain and Europe*, 3rd edn, London, Collins, 1974, pp. 103-4).

3   *Crimson moon*   Baillie wrote [to *Thomson*], 'I meant this to express the kind of arched spot of deep red that is over the eyes of this bird but as I never really saw the bird but once a long time ago, and take my account of him from a book, it may probably not be sufficiently descriptive' (18 February 1805, BL Add. MS. 35623, f. 257).

15-16   *The rarest . . . away*   Thomson requested that these lines be changed because he found them 'obscure', but Baillie wrote to Thomson that she could not alter these lines 'without taking away all the ease and delicacy. . . .' (18 February 1805, BL Add. MS. 35623, f. 257).

21   *Snowdon's mist*   Baillie wrote to Thomson, 'I could lay my hands upon no tour thro' Wales but that of Gilpin in South Wales up the Wye [William Gilpin, *Observations on the River Wye*, 1782], and therefore . . . alter the names of our rivers and mountains as you please. Snowdon sounds well enough, but it is perhaps too high a mountain for the Black Cock to breed in' (21 June 1804, BL Add. MS. 35623, f. 239). (For habitat, see Note for *Title*).

Song, Written for a Welsh Melody: 'I've No Sheep on the Mountain'

This poem was sent with 'O welcome bat, and owlet grey' in February 1804 to George Thomson. Baillie's 'I've no sheep on the mountain . . .' was published in Thomson's *A Select Collection of Original Welsh Airs*, 2, (1811), p. 58, with music by Beethoven.

1 *boat on the lake* Baillie agreed with Thomson that there are no major lakes in Wales, 'but that this lover of hers, tho' in love with a Welsh woman, might be himself a Cumberland man and that will set everything right' (BL Add. MS. 35623, f. 221).

4 *Llanwellyn* Baillie originally spelt this 'Lanvilling'.

9-12 Baillie originally intended this stanza to be comic:

> The neighbours lament that I'm clownish and shy
> And my limbs are too long and nose is awry.
> I thank you, good neighbours, but so let me be,
> Since the Maid of Lanvilling smiles sweetly on me.
>
> (BL Add. MS. 35623, f. 222)

Thomson persuaded Baillie to drop this stanza and to replace it with two additional more conventional stanzas (BL Add. MS. 35623, f. 230).

Song, Written for a Welsh Air: 'Noh Calenig' or 'The New Year's Gift'

This poem was sent to George Thomson in November 1804 (BL Add. MS. 35623, f. 250), and was published in his *A Select Collection of Original Welsh Airs*, 2 (1811), p. 47.

1 *Elaw* a river in Wales.

9 *I gave thee my part* when they married, he gave her his worldly goods. Baillie notes in a letter that Thomson wanted to refer to the male protagonist as a 'helpmate', but she refused, insisting that readers would know that the couple were married.

Song, Written at Mr Thomson's Request: 'Sweet Power of Song'

George Thomson commissioned this poem as 'a kind of introduction to his Irish melodies'. He published 'Sweet power of song', not as a frontispiece, but second in *Irish Airs*, 1 (1814). Baillie wrote to Thomson: 'I have praised the power of music or rather song upon the heart, and have alluded to the three countries of these kingdoms who have national music and whose airs you have published' (BL Add. MS. 35264, f. 3).

14 *beldame* old woman.

17 *hight* called, named.

18 *tie* marriage vow.

23   *Erin's – Cambria's*   Ireland's or Wales's.

24   *Burns*   Baillie here mentions Robert Burns as representative of the best in Scottish poetry.

Song, Written for an Irish Melody: 'His Boat Comes on the Sunny Tide'

Baillie sent a draft of this poem to George Thomson on 8 May 1810 (BL Add. MS. 35263, f. 318), and it was first published in Thomson's *Irish Airs*, 1 (1814), p. 17.

5   *Shannon*   a river in County Clare, southern Ireland. Baillie wrote to Thomson, 'The river Shannon . . . I have treated as a broad navigable river, as I suppose it is near its junction with the sea . . .' (BL Add. MS. 35263, f. 318).

Song, Written for an Irish Melody: 'The Harper Who Sat on his Green Mossy Seat'

Baillie sent a draft of this poem to Thomson on 19 April 1813 (BL Add. MS. 35264, f. 101). The imaginary speaker is an Irish volunteer serving under British colours abroad. (See Thomson's *Irish Airs*, 2 (1816), p.136.)

1   *harper*   This word was originally 'piper' (BL Add. MS. 35264, f. 220).

9   *holy-day air*   holiday spirit.

18   *tuck*   beat.

20   *fifers*   players of small shrill flutes that accompany drums in some military music.

Song, For an Irish Air: 'The Morning Air Plays on My Face'

Baillie had, in a letter of 1 February 1813, intimated to Thomson that she found the writing of words to traditional music difficult: 'I have frequently told you that I have no pleasure in writing songs, and I am certainly not much in the mood for it at present . . .' (BL Add. MS. 35264, f. 80). Nevertheless, she subsequently sent him drafts of two poems that he had commissioned for two Irish airs. One of these was 'The morning air plays on my face' (19 April 1813, BL Add. MS. 35264, f. 98). This poem, for which the music was arranged by Beethoven, was published in Thomson's *Irish Airs*, 1 (1814), p. 10.

15   *Tray*   a dog.

27   *bourn and brake*   stream and thicket.

Song, For an Irish Air: 'Come, Form We Round a Cheerful Ring'

This poem was published in Thomson's *Irish Airs*, 1 (1814) p. 20.

4   *beldame*   old woman.

5   *sightless*   blind.

6   *faggot*   bundle of sticks or twigs bound together as fuel.

8   *bantling*   young child.

13   *Killarney*   a county in Ireland.

17   *will-o'-the-wisp*   phosphorescent light from methane combustion above marshy ground.

21   *glee*   song for several voices in parts.

Song: 'Come Rouse Thee, Lady Fair'

This song first appeared in Baillie's *Fugitive Verses* (1840) along with 'For Fishermen' under her heading of *Two Songs*. Baillie notes that in 1815 these songs 'were written for Mr H. Siddons, when he wished two of those in *The Beacon* [Baillie's musical drama] to be altered, at the time he was preparing it for representation. That amiable and accomplished man, then Manager of the Edinburgh Theatre, died soon after, and the Drama was never produced.' Henry Siddons (1774-1815) was both actor and theatre manager. He was the son of Mrs Sarah Siddons (1755-1831), the famous actress for whom Baillie wrote 'To Mrs Siddons'.

Song: For Fishermen

For note on 1815 as the date of composition, see preceding poem.

Song, For Mr Struther's The Harp of Caledonia: 'It Was On a Morn When We Were Thrang'

John Struthers (1776-1853) was born at Long Calderwood in Lanarkshire where the Baillie family befriended him. Struthers was a cobbler in Glasgow from the age of fifteen, but Baillie persuaded her close friend, Sir Walter Scott, to help Struthers publish his book of poetry, *The Poor Man's Sabbath, with other Poems* (1804). Joanna Baillie, Anne Hunter and Sir Walter Scott also contributed poems to Struther's anthology of Scots songs, *The Harp of Caledonia* (1819), in which Baillie's 'It was on a morn . . .' was first published, p. 357.

This song satirizes an ageing landlord whose power and money are mocked by the young woman he has set out to woo.

1   *thrang*   busy.

2   *kirn*   churn.

3   *bannocks*   flat oatcakes.

4   *ane . . . chapp't*   someone knocked.

5   *mays sae tight*   maidens so neat or shapely.

6   *bald . . . ween*   bold . . . guess.

8   *e'en*   evening.

9   *docksy auld laird*   lazy old landlord.

10   *blate*   bashful.

12   *crousely ben*   arrogantly in.

13   *o'er'ay [overlay]*   a cravat.

14   *bien*   in good condition.

17   *sae braw*   so fine.

18   *liart pow . . . straikit*   silvery hair . . . stroked.

19   *a body half glaikit*   a person half flirtatiously.

22   *clean*   completely.

25   *pawky*   crafty.

26   *fash . . . gilly*   bother . . . silly girl.

27   *skeigh*   frisky.

28   *fitter for you*   more suitable for your requirements.

32   *landward*   [metaphorically] awkward.

34   *ident*   diligent.

35   *douce . . . boudle*   sedate . . . something of little value.

37   *slight*   cunning.

42   *between Orkney and Tweed o!*   from the islands north of Scotland to the river on the Scotland-England border.

44   *de'il*   devil.

46   *stour banning*   hoarse cursing.

To a Child

This poem was first published in *The New Monthly Magazine* (1821), and subsequently in *A Collection of Poems, Chiefly Manuscript, and From Living Authors*, ed. Joanna Baillie, 1823, pp. 165-6. These stanzas are formal elegiac quatrains, in which the poet sees the unformed child as symbolic of 'hope and change'. The child addressed is probably Baillie's grand-niece, Sophia Milligan, the grand-daughter of her brother, Matthew Baillie and his wife, Sophia, daughter of Dr. Thomas Denham, a London physician. They had two children, Elizabeth (1794-1876) and William (1797-1894). Sophia was the daughter of Elizabeth and William Milligan. Sophia, whom Baillie described as 'a wonderfully precious little personage', stayed with Joanna and Agnes Baillie in Hampstead in April 1821 (letter to Margaret Holford, 11 April 1821, Camden Borough Library Collection).

5   *boots*   avails.

6   *hind*   ploughman or small-holding farmer.

7   *wight*   human being, person.

23   *pelf*   money or wealth.

28   *spell or hornbook*   spelling or lettering book.

Song, Woo'd and Married and a' (Version Taken from an Old Song of That Name)

In reference to 'Woo'd and Married and A'', Baillie expressed exasperation at Thomson for asking her to write yet another song: 'I guess this may be about the 13th time that you have promised to me that the song you asked me to write should be the last . . . I am heartily tired of song-writing which I never at any time did like. I should have stood out sturdily against this last request but for two reasons: first, that I was unwilling that your engraving [a frontispiece that illustrated a wedding for George Thomson's *Collection of Songs*, 3(1822), p. i] should not have something written to correspond with it, and secondly that I wish you to help me a little in a subscription which I am carrying on for the benefit of a friend [Baillie's *Collection of Poems*, 1823]' (letter and draft of 'Woo'd and Married and A' to George Thomson, 27 February 1822, BL Add. MS. 35265, f. 106). Baillie's attitude to the writing of songs was ambivalent, however, since she wrote several more adaptations of traditional Scots songs, a challenge which she took up successfully. An earlier version of 'Woo'd and Married and A' was composed by Alexander Ross, and published in James Johnson's *The Scots Musical Museum*, 1 (1787), p. 10.

2   *snooded*   a ribbon bound round the brow and tied at the back under the hair, worn especially by young unmarried women; a symbol of virginity.

5   *pearlins*   lace trimmings.

6   *plenishing*   household furnishing.

8   *Has e'en right mickle ado*   Has much to do.

14   *glakit*   giddy.

15   *plack*   small copper coin once current in Scotland.

17   *wheel*   spinning-wheel.

22   *havins and tocher*   possessions and dowry.

26   *bairn*   child.

27   *cout*   colt.

29   *trow*   believe.

31   *chiel maun*   fellow must.

33   *douce*   respectable (Cf. 'Kerchief to cover so neat', G. Thomson, ed., *Songs of Scotland*, 3, p. i).

35   *greet*   weep.

38   *weel waled*   well chosen.

39   *toom*   empty.

40   *een*   eyes.

44   *purfles and pearlins*   plumpness and pearls.

45   *ony*   any.

46   *buikit*   recorded in the marriage register.

55   *sine*   then.

56   *maukin*   have.

58   *roose*   flatter.

A November Night's Traveller

Baillie, in rhyming tetrameters, describes travelling in a horse-drawn carriage at night. She and her sister, Agnes, did not keep a horse and carriage, so they usually relied on friends' carriages or, for short journeys, hired a pony-chaise: 'Agnes & I ventured our persons in an old crazy pony chaise on Tuesday evening and went to ... Hendon [four miles away] (letter to Margaret Holford, 7 July 1826, Hampstead Borough Library Collection). This poem was composed especially for *A Collection of Poems Chiefly Manuscript* (1823), edited by Baillie, pp. 290-300.

19   *trow*   believe.

23   *wight*   human being, person.

24   *chaise*   carriage.

26   *ban-dogs*   chained dogs.

28   *ostler*   stableman.

38   *motley*   varicoloured.

39   *mantled*   wearing a loose, sleeveless cloak.

40   *plaid*   long piece of twilled woollen cloth, usually with chequered or tartan pattern, outer article of Highland costume, worn over the shoulder.

43   *peat*   vegetable matter decomposed in water and partly carbonized, used for fuel.

53   *hind*   ploughman or smallholding farmer.

58   *Grammercy*   grant mercy.

59   *cantrips*   spells, charms, tricks.

65   *skathe*   harm.

71   *tarpaulin*   waterproof cloth especially of tarred canvas.

72   *mammoth*   a reference to the large extinct elephant with hairy coat and curved tusks.

74   *bonfire*   On 5 November each year in many areas of Britain, people have lit fires to celebrate the arrest of Guy Fawkes, conspirator in the Gunpowder Plot of 1605 to blow up the Houses of Parliament at Westminster. An effigy of Guy Fawkes is often burned in the bonfire.

80   *Bacchants*   revellers who have been drinking. Bacchus is the god of wine in Greek and Roman mythology.

81   *murgeons*   grimaces.

93   *pewter trencher*   platter of grey alloy of tin with lead or other metal for serving food.

94   *pelf*   wealth.

97   *import*   meaning.

115   *pitchy*   pitch-black.

119   *tipsy artisan*   drunken manual worker.

120   *can*   beermug.

126   *pattened*   wearing pattens, that is, shoes made with thick soles or set on an iron ring for raising the wearer's foot out of the mud.

132-3   *a sloppy shower*   sewerage systems in the eighteenth century were rudimentary, which accounted for wash-water and urine being thrown out of windows on to the street.

136   *rent*   hole.

148   *glamoury*   glamour.

152   *Swan / Boar*   inns beside the road.

161   *coil*   disturbance, noise, fuss.

176   *mazy*   resembling a maze.

178   *turnpike gate*   toll-gate.

186   *vizard*   visor, that is, a movable part of helmet covering face.

216   *cheat*   illusion.

218   *yellow diamonds of Cairngorm*   yellowish semi-precious stones from the Cairngorm mountains in Scotland.

227   *elph*   elf.

229   *glamourie*   glamour.

240   *pollard willows*   willow trees cut back so as to produce close rounded heads of young branches.

Address to a Steam-Vessel

This evocation in heroic couplets of a passenger steamship sailing from the River Clyde across the North Channel to Belfast shows Baillie's awareness of scientific and technological developments which she assesses as partly benefi-cial and partly deleterious. The first steamship made of iron was launched in 1818. This poem was also composed especially for *A Collection of Poems Chiefly Manuscript* (1823), edited by Baillie (pp. 259-64).

7   *tresselled*   seats or benches that are held up by trestles.

45   *'in populous city pent'*   John Milton, *Paradise Lost*, IX, 445. Baillie's allusion here is ironic in the context of Milton's simile which describes Satan's vision of Eve before he seduces her.

52   *colworts*   bushy plants.

54   *Loch Lomond*   a lake near the River Clyde.

62   *Ben*   a mountain, probably Ben Lomond near Loch Lomond.

65   *Clyde*   River Clyde near Glasgow.

66   *Cumra*   an island in the Firth of Clyde.

67   *lichens*   plant organisms composed of fungus and algae in association.

74   *Kittywakes*   'The common or vulgar name of a water bird frequenting that coast' (Baillie's note).

78   *Arran's . . . peaks*   Arran Island hills near the Firth of Clyde that the steam vessel passed on its way to Belfast.

83   *work of sordid skill*   This reference to a cotton mill shows Baillie's reservations about industrialization of the workforce.

86   *marshalled pillars*   cliffs on the Irish coastline.

89   *Pharaoh's army*   The Irish cliffs that are sunk deep into the sea resemble Pharaoh's army slowly drowning in the Red Sea (Exodus: 15: 28).

95   *Watt*   James (1736-1819), a Scot, was employed in the deepening of the Clyde and other rivers and improved the steam engine in various ways.

98   *Davy*   Sir Humphrey (1778-1829), who was a professor of chemistry at the Royal Institution, made advances in the knowledge of chemistry and electro-magnetism.

110   *Columbus*   Christopher (1451-1506) discovered the New World of the Americas on his voyage in 1492.

111   *stinted*   limited.

114   *Magellan*   Ferdinand (1480-1521) whose sailing ship first circumnavigated the world.

117   *grog*   a drink of spirit and water served to sailors.

123   *weeds*   garments.

121-32   Baillie compares the aesthetic beauty of sailing-ships with the mundane quality of steam vessels.

Sir Maurice, A Ballad

'Sir Maurice' was another poem composed especially for *A Collection of Poems Chiefly Manuscript* (1823), edited by Baillie (pp. 311-25). 'Sir Maurice' is the tale of an English girl who, in order to save her father's life, married a Muslim lord. She refused Sir Maurice's attempt to rescue her from the Saracen leader. Baillie, however, did not claim that this ballad is based on historical 'sources sufficiently authentic', as she had claimed in connection with her *Metrical Legends of Exalted Characters* ('Preface', *Metrical Legends of Exalted Characters*, 1821, in *Collected Works*, 1851, p. 706). See also Amanda Gilroy, 'From Here to Alterity: The Geography of Femininity in the Poetry of Joanna Baillie' in *A History of Scottish Women's Writing*, ed. Douglas Gifford and Dorothy

McMillan (Edinburgh, Edinburgh University Press, 1997), for an interpretation of this poem in relation to the heroine's 'cross-dressing and exotic travel' (pp. 147-9).

5   *vassals*   holders of land by feudal tenure, on conditions of homage and allegiance.

32   *seneschal*   steward or major-domo of mediaeval great house.

44   *Acre*   a fort in Lebanon.

73   *liegemen*   faithful followers.

119   *Syrian*   Syria is in the Near East, adjacent to Turkey on the Mediterranean Sea.

123   *Saracen*   Arab or Muslim at the time of the Crusades (Christian expeditions against the Muslims with the intention of converting Muslims to the Christian Faith or driving them out of the holy places).

To Mrs Siddons

This is another poem composed especially for *A Collection of Poems Chiefly Manuscript* (1823), edited by Baillie (pp. 150-3). Baillie regretted that she had not referred in this poem to Sarah Siddons's brother, John Philip Kemble, who had died in 1823, not long after Baillie's volume appeared: 'If the lines I have addressed to Mrs Siddons had not been printed before the account of his [Sarah Siddons's brother's] death had reached us here, I would have contrived to weave in a line to his honour in that little poem, tho' during his life I always considered him as being rather unfriendly to me' (letter to Sir Walter Scott, 2 April 1823, National Library of Scotland, MS. 3896, f. 43).

Title: Mrs Sarah Siddons (1755-1831) was one of the leading actresses of her day whose last performance took place in 1819. Mrs Siddons played the part of Jane de Monfort in Baillie's *De Monfort* (1798) when the play was performed at the *Drury Lane* theatre in 1800. Mrs Siddons lived for a time in Hampstead and visited Joanna Baillie there. In a letter to Sir Walter Scott, Baillie defended Sarah Siddons against his trenchant criticism: 'we shall never see her like again or one approaching within many degrees of her excellence' (28 June 1819, National Library of Scotland, MS 3890, f. 132).

21   *ween*   think.

29   Joanna Baillie's note: 'Those who have been happy enough to hear Mrs Siddons read, will readily acknowledge that the discrimination and power with which she gave effect to the comic passages of Shakespeare, were nearly as remarkable and delightful as those which she displayed in passages of a grave or tragic character. It is to be regretted that only those who have heard her read are aware of the extent or variety of her genius, which has on the stage been

confined almost entirely to tragedy; partly, I believe, from a kind of bigotry on the side of the public, which inclines it to confine poet, painter, or actor, to that department of their art in which they have first been acknowledged to excel, and partly from the cast of her features, and the majesty of her figure being particularly suited to tragedy.'

36   *Who hath so long in Stratford's chancel*   Shakespeare's monument in Stratford church.

38   Baillie, in the same letter to Sir Walter Scott, added that she disagreed with his criticisms of the great actress, 'I think you are hard upon the elder and great Mrs Siddons. . . . she has a mind which has been occupied in observing what passed within itself, and has therefore drawn her acting from a deeper source than actors generally do, besides her native talent for expressing emotions . . .' (28 June 1819, National Library of Scotland, MS. 3890, f. 132).

51   *wight*   fellow.

55   *saloon*   public hall or large room for assemblies.

Hooly and Fairly (Founded on an Old Scottish Song)

This poem is an adaptation of 'The Drucken [Drunken] Wife of Gallowa', a song which first appeared in *The Charmer* (1751), authorship unknown. Baillie's adaptation, which is in the first person voice of a naive man, is a satiric expose of his inability to adjust to the behaviour of his spirited, if somewhat vulgar, wife. It was first published in Thomson's *Collection of Songs*, 4 (1822).

Title: slowly and gently.

2   *posset and wine o' Canary*   cheap rough wine and sweet wine from the Canary Islands.

3   *thraw-gabbit cairly*   peevish old woman.

7   *kimmers*   wenches or gossips.

14   *buskit sae braw*   dresses so handsomely.

15   *mantuas*   bonnets made or as made in Mantua, Italy;   *gar me gae barely* make me go without.

20   *babs o' red roses and breast-knots o'erlaid*   bunches of red roses and ribbons embroidered on her clothes.

21   *The Dominie stickit the psalm very nearly*   the minister almost missed the psalm.

25   *flyting*   scolding.

27   *nieve*   fist;   *sairly*   grievously, harshly.

31   *cantrips*   frolics.

32   *chaumer unred*   bedroom in disorder.

38   *Elders*   in the Church of Scotland (which is Presbyterian), persons elected or ordained to take part in church government.

39   *text she flings rarely [rairly]*   with a roar, throws his biblical quotation back at him.

44   *doited*   feeble-minded.

45   *in the mouls*   turned mouldy.

46   *what does it 'vail*   George Thomson changed this line to 'what does't avail' (BL Add. MS. 35265, f. 110), but Baillie did not accept this alteration.

A Scottish Song: 'The Gowan Glitters on the Sward'

Baillie sent this poem to Thomson on 16 December 1811 (BL Add. MS. 35264, f. 58), and it was published in Thomson's *Collection of Songs*, 4 (1822). Baillie commented, 'Being Scotch music ['The Shepherd's Son'], I have written Scotch words for it; not the old Scotch, but such Scotch as is still spoken in the country.'

1   *gowan . . . sward*   daisy . . . turf.

2   *lavrock*   skylark.

3   *collie . . . ward*   sheepdog . . . watch.

7   *trysting*   making an assignation.

15   *ghaist*   ghost.

16   *croon*   sing in a low tone.

19   *Lucky*   a grandmother.

20   *bairnies*   children.

25   *I cost yestreen, frae Chapman Tom*   I bought yesterday from pedlar Tom.

26   *snood*   hair ribbon.

30   *mark it winna' pass*   darkness will not.

34   *knowe*   knoll.

35   *Browny's brae*   goblin's hillside.

36   *lowe*   state of ardour.

38   *glamrie*   witchcraft / deception.

41   *book o' grace*   Bible.

42   *conn'd*   studied.

46   *gane*   gone.

48   *ony stane*   any stone.

Song, For a Scottish Air: 'O Swiftly Glides the Bonny Boat'

Baillie apologized to George Thomson for her not responding promptly to his earlier request for another song, 'I had too long neglected to answer a letter of yours which I received a long time ago; containing a request which, though an unexpected one, yet being a *last*, I did not mean to refuse. Various engagements and occupations have since prevented me from fulfilling my intention, but this morning I have at last found leisure for it, and enclose a boat song which I have tried to make something like what I suppose you desired. I hope it will in some degree please you, and that it does not reach you too late to be of use. I have followed the measure of the pattern verses ['O Weel May the Boatie Row' by John Ewen (1741-1821)] for I don't recollect the air nor have I anybody near me to play it to me. I flatter myself, however, that the verses I have written are of a character not unsuited to the music.' This poem was published in Thomson's *Collection of Songs*, 5 (1822).

Chorus: 'If nets cannot be said with propriety to float as they are dragged down by the lead while the pieces of cork only are seen upon the water, let the second line of the Chorus run thus: "Our nets are circled wide"' (letter to George Thomson, 20 July 1817, BL Add. MS. 35264, f. 305). Cf. John Ewen's version in George Farquhar Graham, ed., *The Popular Songs of Scotland* (Glasgow, J. M. Wood, 1887), pp. 224-5:

> I cuist my line in Largo bay,
> And fishes I caught nine.
> There's three to boil, and three to fry,
> And three to bait the line.
> The boatie rows, the boatie rows,
> The boatie rows indeed;
> And happy be the lot of a'
> That wish the boatie speed.

Song, For a Scottish Air: 'Poverty Parts Good Company'

This song was based on the melody of 'Todlin Hame', and published in Thomson's *Collection of Songs*, 2 (1822). Thomson prefaced it with the following note, which Baillie disliked. This note read: 'It affords peculiar satisfaction to the Editor, to have obtained these uncommonly beautiful verses for one of the most pleasing of the Scottish Melodies – a Melody to which he must ever be partial, from a recollection of the matchless way in which it was sung by the most exhilerating of all Scottish youngsters, the late Mr. James Balfour.' Thomson took no notice of Baillie's objection, but instead altered the words 'uncommonly beautiful verses' to 'exquisitely beautiful verses' in his 1838 edition.

1   *o'erlay*   cravat.

2   *siller*   silver.

3   *brae*   hillside.

4   *cleeding*   clothing.

8   *crusie*   open, boat-shaped lamp.

15   *een*   eyes.

17   *Mertimass*   Feast of St Martin (11 November).

21   *bridal and infare, I braced me*   at wedding and reception, I girded myself [metaphorically].

22   *bruise*   a foot-race from the wedding to the reception.

25   *dowie and dree*   sad and dreary.

28   *unco*   very.

29   *Kebbuck and beeker*   cheese and large drinking-cup.

31   *slee*   sly.

34   *spae-wife*   fortune-teller.

35   *loof*   palm.

37   *ilka*   every.

Song: 'Fy, Let Us A' to the Wedding' (An Auld Sang, New Buskit)

Baillie adapted at the request of George Thomson, 'Fy, let us a' to the wedding' from 'The Blythesome Bridal' which begins, 'Fy, let us a' to the bridal' (James Watson, ed., *Choice Collection of Scots Poems*, 1706-1711). She used the opening stanzas verbatim but subsequently altered the names and the idiosyncrasies of the wedding guests. Baillie thus satirizes several types of people she had known in Lanarkshire, Scotland. She was ambivalent, however, about her adaptation: 'I at first felt somewhat angry that you should wish to disturb our old popular ballad of "Fy let us all to the wedding", and thought that nothing put in its place would have any chance of pleasing my Northern countrymen; but some time afterwards it suddenly came into my head that it might be managed without giving them offence. . . . The character of the old song is preserved, for I would not think of altering that, yet I question whether the admirers of the old rigmarole with all its pithy nicknames will give me any thanks for what I have done . . .' (letter to George Thomson, 23 January 1827, BL Add. MS. 35265, f. 182). This poem is reprinted from Baillie's *Fugitive Verses* (1840), pp. 275-80. The first two stanzas of 'Fy Let Us A' to the Bridal' are:

> Fy let us a' to the bridal
> For there will be lilting there
> For Jocky's to be married to Maggie
> The lass wi' the gowden hair.
> And there will be langkail and pottage,
> And bannocks of barley-meal,
> And there will be good sawt herring,
> To relish a cog of good ale.
>
> And there will be Saney the Sutor
> And Will wi' the meikle mow;
> And there will be Tam the blutter
> With Andrew the tinker I trow;
> And there will be bow'd legged Robie,
> With thumbless Katie's goodman;
> And there will be blue-cheeked Dowbie,
> And Lawrie the laird of the land.

(From Douglas Herd, ed., *Ancient and Modern Scottish Songs* [1769] vol. 2, pp. 161-4). Cf. Robert Burns, 'The Election: A New Song' which is a satirical poem with the same stanzaic form and metre as 'Fy Let Us A' to the Bridal', but set in a political context (see *The Poems and Songs of Robert Burns*, ed. James Kinsley, vol. 3, pp. 777-80).

Title: *buskit*   prepared.

5   *jibing and jeering*   taunting and deriding.

6   *een*   eyes.

7   *smooth-gabbit speering*   smooth-tongued prying.

8   *pawky*   crafty, sly.

10   *cockup*   pad of false hair to heighten a coiffure.

12   *gang na'ajee*   goes not awry.

14   *coft*   bought.

16   *dowie and cow'd*   dismal and intimidated.

18   *perk at the top of the ha'*   preen at the top of the hall.

21   *cleckit*   invented.

22   *haver and glower*   talk foolishly and stare.

23   *tocherless maids*   dowryless maids.

25   *clavering*   gossiping.

27   *vaunty*   proud.

28   *to caird*   to card wool (i.e. her aunt teaches her nothing useful).

30   *clerical blade*   dashing young clergyman.

32   *coof*   stupid.

34   *thrity and twa*   thirty-two.

35   *thraw gabbit*   loud-mouthed.

37   *sewster sae genty*   seamstress so neat.

38   *havens*   deportment.

39   *straik*   smooth down.

40   *crack wi' Mess John i' the spence*   gossip with the church minister in the inner room.

41   *fairlies*   marvels.

43   *bogles*   ghosts.

49   *town writer*   town-lawyer.

52   *after-grist*   profit.

55   *vilipend*   vilifying.

59   *ha'ding*   farm-holding.

62   *browst*   brew (malt liquor).

65   *florentines*   meatpies.

67   *chuckies*   chickens.

68   *pat*   pot.

72   *Dumbuck*   a small village near the River Clyde.

73   *daffing*   romping.

74   *reeling*   dancing in a set formation.

76   *aumry*   pantry.

79   *skirling*   making a shrill sound.

80   *lin*   waterfall.

Verses Written in February, 1827

This poem, which is in heroic couplets, and castigates those in Britain who treat horses inhumanely, was published in *Fugitive Verses* (1840), pp. 230-3. In 1826, Baillie wrote and had printed a fifteen-page pamphlet, *A Lesson Intended for the Use of the Hampstead School*, on the prevention of cruelty to animals.

21   *lean galled sides*   thin sorely chafed horses.

Song, To the Scottish Air of 'My Nanny O'

These words are based on a traditional lyric; Cf. Robert Burns's 'My Nanie O' in *The Poems and Songs of Robert Burns*, ed. James Kinsley, vol. 2, pp. 7-9, who notes that 'The earliest publication of My Nanie O' is in *Orpheus Caledonius*, 1725, No. 38, vol. 3, p. 1007.' According to Baillie, Burns's version is 'plaintive', whereas hers has a satiric note in her characterization of the first-person speaker, a young man. (See *Fugitive Verses* (1840), p.138.)

1   *bruise*   Baillie's spelling of 'broose', which means a foot-race at a Scottish country wedding from the church ceremony to the reception party.

2   *wan*   won.

3   *blouzing*   blushing.

7   *sinsyne*   long since.

8   *list*   desire.

10   *wad fain . . . canna'o*   would gladly be sedate / respectable but cannot.

11   *muir or craft*   moor or croft.

12   *sa blithe*   so joyous.

17   *mither scolds*   mother scolds.

21   *spae-wife on my loof*   the fortune-teller on my palm.

22   *leeing ranny*   lying beggarwoman.

23   *weel kens*   well knows.

The Merry Bachelor (Founded on the Old Scottish Song, 'Willie Was a Wanton Wag')

This poem is also based on a traditional Scottish song, 'Wanton Willie', which is referred to in *The Poems and Songs of Robert Burns*, ed. James Kinsley, vol. 2, p. 930. (See *Fugitive Verses* (1840), pp.184-6.)

1   *wanton wag*   jovial practical joker.

3   *brag*   challenge.

4   *carried a' the gree*   won first place.

5   *stark and keen*   vigorous and courageous.

6   *gaed to the weapon-shaw*   went to a periodical review of men under arms.

9   *liel*   [leal] loyal.

15   *wan the bruise*   [broose] a race at a country wedding from the church to the reception.

18   *buskit braw*   dressed splendidly.

23   *gloom*   frown, scowl.

24   *blitheness*   cheerfulness

25   *Mess John*   Presbyterian minister (jocular);   *laive*   love.

26   *dominie . . . lair*   the schoolmaster for all his learning.

30   *ilka*   every.

33   *carlin*   old woman.

37   *main*   seas.

40   *doufness*   melancholy.

Song, *A New Version of an Old Scottish Song: 'Saw Ye Johnny Comin''*

This poem was first published in *Fugitive Verses* (1840). In a letter to George Thomson, Baillie referred to it as 'Fee him, father, fee him', which she said that she 'wrote for Miss Head of Ashfield of Devonshire . . . many years ago' (letter to Thomson, 1 May 1841, BL Add. MS. 35265, f. 286). Thomson had printed this poem without attribution in *Fifty Scottish Songs with Symphonies and Accompaniments by Haydn*, Vol. 3, p. 10. In 1841, he wished to reprint this poem with acknowledgement of Baillie as author.

3   *bonnet*   a soft flat brimless cap worn by men and boys.

5   *gloamin'*   evening twilight.

10   *fee*   hire.

16   *merks o' geer*   goods in exchange.

17   *rue*   regret.

19   *hizzy*   frivolous woman.

21   *sark*   shirt.

23   *kist*   chest, trunk.

25   *merk o' mair fee*   more money to hire him.

27   *dinna stand wi'*   do not be reluctant about.

30   *brawest*   finest.

31   *haverels*   half-wits.

33   *dowie*   sad.

34   *thrash*   beat corn.

35   *crack*   gossip, talk.

Verses to Our Own Flowery Kirtled Spring

These stanzas (1840) in heroic couplets are a conventional address to spring.

Title: *Kirtled*   dressed.

11   *bedight*   adorned.

44   *wight*   person.

100   *sere*   [sear] withered, dried up.

School Rhymes for Negro Children

The use of the word 'Negro' might be disliked by some readers today, but was polite in the early eighteenth century. In her description, in sestets, of the imaginative play of black children in the tropics, Baillie uses vivid images such as 'dance to their shadows upon the wall' (1840).

Rhymes for Chanting

These rhymes (1840) were written for children at the Hampstead School.

The Country Lady's Reveillie

In a letter to Dr John Clarke-Whitfield (1770-1836), composer and organist, Baillie wrote formally in the third person that she recognized 'the great honour he has done to her verses by joining them to such beautiful music . . . the song "From early fire wending" may be called "the Lady's Reveillie"' (15 July 1815, BL Add. MS. 40856, f. 90). Baillie gave this poem the title, 'The Country Lady's Reveillie', in *Fugitive Verses* (1840), pp. 309-10.

Title: *Reveillie*   a call to wake up.

17   *are bracing*   are fastening belts.

23   *sheeling*   [shieling] a hut for dairymaids on a high or remote summer pasture.

Song: 'Bird Soaring High'

This poem, which was published in *Fugitive Verses* (1840), is written in a male voice, which is a period convention that women poets often followed when treating the theme of love.

4   *frith*   archaic version of *firth*, an estuary.

8   *palfrey*   saddlehorse for riding.

Song: 'What Voice Is This, Thou Evening Gale'

This poem was published in *Fugitive Verses* (1840), pp. 369-70.

12   *motioned love the measure keep*   love is metaphorically a dance.

15   *list*   listen.

16   *The dead*   The speaker's lover is dead, but lives on in her memory.

Lines to Agnes Baillie on Her Birthday

This poem in heroic couplets is addressed to Baillie's sister, who was older by two years, and with whom she lived all her life. Agnes survived Joanna by ten years, dying just before she turned one hundred. This poem, which was probably composed in 1825, was published in *Fugitive Verses* (1840), pp. 219-25. Cf. William Cowper's 'On the Receipt of my Mother's Picture out of Norfolk' (1798), which, although it is elegiac, is a forerunner to poems of Romantic sensibility about family affections.

14   *par*   a fish.

43   *bootless*   unavailing.

113   *he*   their brother, Matthew, who was a year older than Joanna.

115   *wight*   person.

120   *mite*   modest contribution.

122   *lay*   poem.

Select Verses from the 147th Psalm

In 1824, Baillie was commissioned by the Reverend Principal Baird of the University of Edinburgh to write metrical versions of psalms along the lines of *Translations and Paraphrases, in Verse, of Several Passages of Sacred Scripture* (1781). Baillie had reservations about undertaking this work, 'I feel, however, great misgivings as to the success that may attend it; for to alter any of the venerable & simple expressions of scripture for the sake of rhyme and measure has always gone against my feelings and this strong impression will stand like a Lion in the path & make me afraid to proceed' (letter to Principal Baird, 16 January 1824, National Library of Scotland, MS 3435, f. 129). Baillie wrote metrical versions of Matthew 5: 9, Luke 18: 16, John 21: 1, Luke 7: 12, Job 13: 15, and 'Thoughts Taken from the 93rd Psalm' as well as 'Select Verses from the 147th Psalm'. Six months later, Baillie wrote to Baird on 5 June 1824, 'I am very glad to learn by your very obliging letter that the pieces I formerly sent to you for the Scotch Psalmody are of the kind which you think may suit the intentions of the [Presbyterian] Assembly' (National Library of Scotland, MS 3436, f. 144). Although subsequently Principal Baird did not publish any of Baillie's hymns or psalms, she printed them in her *Fugitive Verses* (1840), pp. 373-407. 'Select Verses from the 147th Psalm' is on p. 406.

Hymn: 'My Soul! And Dost Thou Faintly Shrink'

This hymn was one of those commissioned by Principal Baird and published in Baillie's *Fugitive Verses* (1840), p. 383.

36   *welkin*   sky

39-41   *Eye hath . . . who love Him*   1 Corinthians 2: 9.

Recollections of a Dear and Steady Friend

This poem was probably begun after 1816, the year in which Lord Byron separated from his wife, Lady Anne Isabella Milbanke (1792-1860). The poem was first published in *Dramatic and Poetical Works*, pp. 808-10.

Title: The *friend* referred to in the title is Lady Anne Isabella Milbanke who was the daughter of Joanna Baillie's friend, Baroness Judith Wentworth (1777-1822), who married Sir Ralph Milbanke (1747-1825). Anne Isabella Milbanke married Lord George Gordon Byron (1788-1824), sixth baron, politician, and poet, in 1815, and had on daughter, Ada, by him. At that time Byron, who was one of the board of managers at the Drury Lane theatre, tried to have Baillie's drama, *De Monfort*, performed on stage, but his efforts failed. When he separated from his wife in 1816, Baillie sided with his wife in her castigation of

Byron's rumored sexual misconduct. Baillie even tried to prevail on Sir Walter Scott to persuade Byron to return some of his former wife's money to her after their separation, but Byron did not give back any of his wife's inheritance to her.

21   *moody*   an allusion to Thomas Babington Macaulay's epithet for the 'Byronic hero' (1830).

45   *weary of the gossip*   In 1824, Thomas Medwin's *Journal of the Conversations of Lord Byron: Noted During a Residence with his Lordship in Pisa, in the Years 1821 and 1822*, appeared. In a letter to Lady Bentham, Baillie defended her friend, Lady Byron: 'It [Medwin's *Journal*] contains many falsehoods, some of them to the injury of poor Lady Byron, who never did, and was totally incapable of doing what has been ascribed to her. She is our near-neighbour at present and in bad health, and we grieve to think that a creature so excellent in disposition & conduct (for I have known her intimately for many years & love & esteem her most perfectly) should be so annoyed by the baseness of such publication' (8 November 1824, BL Add. MSS 33546, f. 24).

47   *unusual silence*   Baillie defended Lady Byron to Sir Walter Scott, 'There is nothing which the world can pretend to censure in Lady Byron but that she is supposed to be of a very cold & unforgiving nature. That she is a woman of great self-command I know; and where this is the case we cannot well judge of the degree of feeling; but I never in the whole course of my life met with any person of a more candid & forgiving disposition. She has borne treatment & wrongs exceeding anything I have ever heard in married life, and could she [have] hoped for any amendment in his character, or even without this hope, could she have continued to live with him without becoming herself worthless & debased, she would I am confident never have left him (letter to Sir Walter Scott, 21 February 1817, National Library of Scotland, MS. 3888, f. 37). Cf. Baillie's comment in a letter to Margaret Holford: '. . . she [Lady Byron] suffers with a pious, meek, & cheerful mind except when occasional fits of depression come over her . . .' (21 November 1825, Camden Borough Library collection).

66   *Mary Millicent Montgomery*   she is often referred to as 'MM' in Lady Byron's correspondence and diary.

89   *Mistress at length of wealth and large domain*   When Byron died in 1824, his wife inherited his property and what remained of his wealth.

The Weary Pund o' Tow

There seems to be no record extant of this Scots English poem being commissioned or published by George Thomson, but this version of a traditional Scottish song was published in Baillie's *Dramatic and Poetical Works* (1851),

p. 821. This ballad concerns a young housewife who finds her duty of spinning flax is very tiresome. (Cf. 'The Weary Pund of Tow' in *The Poems and Songs of Robert Burns*, ed. James Kinsley, Vol. 2, pp. 622-3.)

4   *ferlie*   a piece of surprising news.

5   *weary pund o' tow*   dispiriting pound of flax or hemp fibre.

6   *lyart pow*   white or silver head of hair.

9   *chapman wi' his gear*   fellow with his goods.

13   *may*   maid.

21   *crooning*   low humming.

25   *webs*   woven pieces of cloth.

26   *linkum twine*   briskly spun yarn.

27   *burn*   stream.

33   *sarkless*   shirtless.

Tam o' the Lin

This Scots English poem was also neither published nor commissioned by George Thomson, but appeared in Baillie's *Dramatic and Poetical Works* (1851), pp. 821-2. The eponymous hero is represented in a similar manner to that of 'Hooly and Fairly', except that the tale is narrated in the third person with occasional pieces of dialogue. Tam is shown to be full of his own self-importance, but marriage leads to a terminal depression. Here Baillie is satirizing complacency in men, as well as subtly mocking the institution of marriage.

1   *Lin*   waterfall.

3   *deil-haet*   devilish.

4   *daur*   dare.

5   *mear*   mare.

8   *yaud*   a worn out mare.

9   *may*   maid.

11   *jerkin*   sleeveless jacket.

12   *laird*   landlord.

14   *chapman*   pedlar.

17   *lare*   [lear] learning.

20   *Dominie*   schoolmaster.

21   *wi' ae horn*   with one horn.

24   *reiver*   plunderer.

28   *bailie*   person in charge of cows on a farm.

29   *dowie and douce*   dull and sober.

31   *chield*   fellow.

35   *masses*   celebrations of the Eucharist.

36   *latewake*   the frequently large and riotous gathering over a corpse until burial or after burial.

New Words to the Old Scottish Air of 'The Wee Pickle Tow'

Although George Thomson invited Baillie to write a version of this poem for his *Collection of Scottish Poems*, Baillie declined, writing to Thomson, 'I am pleased that you should still suppose that I have spirit enough to deal with your Auld Wife and her wee pickle tow, but I do not feel that I have . . .' (BL Add. MS. 35265, 30 March 1842, f. 320). Nevertheless, Baillie must have changed her mind and written a version which she never sent to Thomson, since he did not publish it. This poem was published in Baillie's *Dramatic and Poetical Works* (1851), pp. 822-3, and tells the story of a girl whose distaff for spinning caught fire in a mysterious manner.

1   *wee pickle tow*   small bits of flax or hemp fibre.

3   *rock took a low*   distaff caught fire (literally); *low* means also a state of ardour or excitement, or a blaze of feeling (figuratively).

5   *ween*   think.

6   *mischanter*   misadventure.

7   *keen*   fierce.

8   *dole*   evil, malice.

10   *mon' she crooket*   she blamed her man for her misfortune.

11   *fell*   fierce.

12   *sain*   severely.

13   *Foul fa' . . . o'rock and o'reel*   May the inventor of distaff and spinning reel fall foul of the plague.

15   *wot I weel*   know I well.

17   *kemping*   striving, competing.

21   *doited . . . fou'*   stupid . . . drunk.

22   *dowie*   dull, dismal.

23   *louve-pouther*   love powder.

25   *unchancy*   unlucky.

27   *warlock*   wizard, magician, male equivalent of a witch.

29   *Spunkie*   will-o'-the-wisp;   *boggie*   [boggle] terrifying ghost or phantom.

30   *lunzie folk . . . kirtle*   fairy folk . . . woman's gown.

Appendix 1

'Introductory Discourse' from A Series of Plays (1798)

This is the first section (pp. 1-26) of Joanna Baillie's 'Preface' to *A Series of Plays* (1798), which she published anonymously. In 'Introductory Discourse', Baillie sets out her theories of dramatic art. She recognizes that everyone is interested in determining the 'character' of other individuals: 'Every person, who is not deficient in intellect, is more or less occupied in tracing, amongst the individuals he converses with, the varieties of understanding and temper which constitute the characters of men; and receives great pleasure from every stroke of nature that points out to him those varieties.' Thus, she suggests, works of art, including drama, the novel, and poetry, should be concerned with the feelings and behaviour of the common man and woman rather than with the 'artificial', cultivated feelings 'of the more refined part of society'.

It is natural for a writer, who is about to submit his works to the public, to feel a strong inclination, by some Preliminary Address, to conciliate the favour of his reader, and dispose him, if possible, to peruse them with a favourable eye. I am well aware, however, that his endeavours are generally fruitless: in his situation our hearts revolt from all appearance of confidence, and we consider his diffidence as hypocrisy. Our own word is frequently taken for what we say of ourselves, but very rarely for what we say of our works. Were these three plays, which this small volume contains, detached pieces only, and unconnected with others that do not yet appear, I should have suppressed this inclination altogether; and have allowed my reader to begin what is before him, and to form what opinion of it his taste or his humour might direct, without any previous trespass upon his time or his patience. But they are part of an extensive design: of one which, as far as my information goes, has nothing exactly similar to it in any language: of one which a whole lifetime will be limited enough to accomplish; and which has, therefore, a considerable chance of being cut short by that hand which nothing can resist.

Before I explain the plan of this work, I must make a demand upon the patience of my reader, whilst I endeavour to communicate to him those ideas regarding human nature, as they in some degree affect almost every species of moral writings, but particularly the dramatic, that induced me to attempt it; and, as far as my judgement enabled me to apply them, has directed me in the execution of it.

From that strong sympathy which most creatures, but the human above all, feel for others of their kind, nothing has become so much an object of man's curiosity as man himself. We are all conscious of this within ourselves, and so constantly do we meet with it in others, that like every circumstance of continually repeated occurrence, it thereby escapes observation. Every person, who is not deficient in intellect, is more or less occupied in tracing, among the individuals he converses with, the varieties of understanding and temper which constitute the characters of men; and receives great pleasure from every stroke of nature that points out to him those varieties. This is, much more than we are aware of, the occupation of children, and of grown people also, whose penetration is but lightly esteemed; and that conversation which degenerates with them into trivial and mischievous tattling, takes its rise not infrequently from the same source that supplies the rich vein of the satirist and the wit. That eagerness so universally shown for the conversation of the latter, plainly enough indicates how many people have been occupied in the same way with themselves. Let anyone, in a large company, do or say what is strongly expressive of his peculiar character, or of some passion or humour of the moment, and it will be detected by almost every person present. How often may we see a very stupid countenance animated with a smile, when the learned and the wise have betrayed some native feature of their own minds! and how often will this be the case when they have supposed it to be concealed under a very sufficient disguise! From this constant employment of their minds, most people, I believe, without being conscious of it, have stored up in idea the greater part of those strong marked varieties of human character, which may be said to divide it into classes; and in one of those classes they involuntarily place every new person they become acquainted with.

I will readily allow that the dress and the manners of men, rather than their characters and disposition are the subjects of our common conversation, and seem chiefly to occupy the multitude. But let it be remembered that is is much easier to express our observations on these. It is easier to communicate to another how a man wears his wig and cane, what kind of house he inhabits, and what kind of table he keeps, than from what slight traits in his words and actions we have been led to conceive certain impressions of his character: traits that will often escape the memory, when the opinions that were founded upon them remain. Besides, in communicating our ideas of the characters of others, we are often called upon to support them with more expense of reasoning than we can well afford, but our observations on the dress and appearance of men seldom involve us in such difficulties. For these, and other reasons too tedious to mention, the generality of people appear to us more trifling than they are: and I may venture to say that, but for this sympathetic curiosity towards others of our kind, which is so strongly implanted within us, the attention we pay to the dress and the manners of men would dwindle into an employment as insipid as examining the varieties of plants and minerals is to one who understands not natural history.

In our ordinary intercourse with society, this sympathetic propensity of our minds is exercised upon men, under the common occurrences of life, in which we have often observed them. Here vanity and weakness put themselves forward to view, more conspicuously than the virtues: here men encounter those smaller trials, from which they are not apt to come off victorious; and here, consequently, that which is marked with the whimsical and ludicrous will strike us most forcibly, and make the strongest impression on our memory. To this sympathetic propensity of our minds, so exercised, the genuine and pure comic of every composition, whether drama, fable, story, or satire is addressed.

If man is an object of so much attention to man, engaged in the ordinary occurrences of life, how much more does he excite his curiosity and interest when placed in extraordinary situations of difficulty and distress? It cannot be any pleasure we receive from the sufferings of a fellow-creature which attracts such multitudes of people to a public execution, though it is the horror we conceive for such a spectacle that keeps so many more away. To see a human being bearing himself up under such circumstances, or struggling with the terrible apprehensions which such a situation impresses, must be the powerful incentive, which makes us press forward to behold what we shrink from, and wait with trembling expectation for what we dread.[1] For though few at such a spectacle can get near enough to distinguish the expression of face, or the minuter parts of a criminal's behaviour, yet from a considerable distance will they eagerly mark whether he steps firmly; whether the motions of his body denote agitation or calmness; and if the wind does but ruffle his garment, they will, even from that change upon the outline of his distant figure, read some expression connected with his dreadful situation. Though there is a greater proportion of people in whom this strong curiosity will be overcome by other dispositions and motives; though there are many more who will stay away from such a sight than will go to it; yet there are very few who will not be eager to converse with a person who has beheld it; and to learn, very minutely, every circumstance connected with it, except the very act itself of inflicting death. To lift up the roof of his dungeon, like the *Diable boiteux*,[2] and look upon a criminal the night before he suffers, in his still hours of privacy, when all that disguise, which respect for the opinion of others, the strong motive by which even the lowest and wickedest of men still continue to be moved, would present an object to the mind of every person, not withheld from it by great timidity of character, more powerfully attractive than almost any other.

Revenge, no doubt, first began amongst the savages of America that dreadful custom of sacrificing their prisoners of war. But the perpetuation of such hideous cruelty could never have become a permanent national custom, but for this universal desire in the human mind to behold man in every situation, putting forth his strength against the current of adversity, scorning all bodily anguish, or struggling with those feelings of nature, which, like a beating stream, will ofttimes burst through the artificial barriers of pride. Before they begin those terrible rites they treat their prisoner kindly; and it cannot be supposed that men, alternately enemies and friends to so many neighbouring tribes, in manners and appearance like themselves, should so strongly be actuated by a spirit of public revenge. This custom, therefore, must be considered as a grand and terrible game, which every tribe plays against another; where they try not the strength of the arm, the swiftness of the feet, nor the acuteness of the eye, but the fortitude of the soul. Considered in this light, the excess of cruelty exercised upon their miserable victim, in which every hand is described as ready to inflict its portion of pain, and every head ingenious in the contrivance of it, is no longer to be wondered at. To put into his measure of misery one agony less, would be, in some degree, betraying the honour of their nation: would be doing a species of injustice to every hero of their own tribe who had already sustained it, and to those who might be called upon to do so; amongst whom each of these savage tormentors has his chance of being one, and has prepared himself for it from his childhood. Nay, it would be a species of injustice to the haughty victim himself, who would scorn to purchase his place amongst the heroes of his nation, at an easier price than his undaunted predecessors.

Amongst the many trials to which the human mind is subjected, that of holding intercourse, real or imaginary, with the world of spirits: of finding itself alone with a being terrific and awful, whose nature and power are unknown, has been justly considered as one of the most severe. The workings of nature in this situation, we all know, have ever been the object of our most eager enquiry. No man wishes to see the ghost himself, which would certainly procure him the best information on the subject, but every man wishes to see one who believes that he sees it, in all the agitation and wildness of that species of terror. To gratify this curiosity how many people have dressed up hideous apparitions to frighten the timid and superstitious! And have done it at the risk of destroying their happiness or understanding forever. For the instances of intellect being destroyed by this kind of trial are more numerous, perhaps, in proportion to the few who have undergone it than by any other.

How sensible we are of this strong propensity within us, when we behold any person under the pressure of great and uncommon calamity! Delicacy and respect for the afflicted will, indeed, make us turn ourselves aside from observing him, and cast down our eyes in his presence; but the first glance we direct to him will involuntarily be one of the keenest observation, how hastily soever it may be checked; and often will a returning look of enquiry mix itself by stealth with our sympathy and reserve.

But it is not in situations of difficulty and distress alone, that man becomes the object of this sympathetic curiosity; he is no less so when the evil he contends with arises in his own breast, and no outward circumstance connected with him either awakens our attention or our pity. What human creature is there, who can behold a being like himself under the violent agitation of those passions which all have, in some degree experienced without feeling himself most powerfully excited by the sight? I say, all have experienced; for the bravest man on earth knows what fear is as well as the coward; and will not refuse to be interested for one under the dominion of this passion, provided there be nothing in the circumstances attending it to create contempt. Anger is a passion that attracts less sympathy than any other, yet the unpleasing and distorted features of an angry man will be more eagerly gazed upon, by those

who are no wise concerned with his fury or the objects of it, than the most amiable placid countenance in the world. Every eye is directed to him; every voice
hushed to silence in his presence; even children will leave off their gambols as
he passes, and gaze after him more eagerly than the gaudiest equipage. The
wild tossings of despair; the gnashing of hatred and revenge; the yearnings of
affection, and the softened mien of love; all that language of the agitated soul,
which every age and nation understands, is never addressed to the dull nor
inattentive.

It is not merely under the violent agitations of passion that man so arouses
and interests us; even the smallest indication of an unquiet mind, the restless
eye, the muttering lip, the half-checked exclamation, and the hasty start, will
set our attention as anxiously upon the watch as the first distant flashes of a
gathering storm. When some great explosion of passion bursts forth, and some
consequent catastrophe happens, if we are at all acquainted with the unhappy
perpetrator, how minutely will we endeavour to remember every circumstance
of his past behaviour! and with what avidity will we seize upon every recollected
word or gesture, that is in the smallest degree indicative of the supposed state
of his mind, at the time when they took place. If we are not acquainted with
him, how eagerly will we listen to similar recollections from another! Let us
understand, from observation or report, that any person harbours in his breast,
concealed from the world's eye, some powerful rankling passion of what kind
soever it may be, we will observe every word, every motion, every look, even
the distant gait of such a man, with a constancy and attention bestowed upon
no other. Nay, should we meet him unexpectedly on our way, a feeling will
pass across our minds as though we found ourselves in the neighbourhood of
some secret and fearful thing. If invisible, would we not follow him into his
lonely haunts, into his closet, into the midnight silence of his chamber? There
is, perhaps, no employment which the human mind will with so much avidity
pursue, as the discovery of concealed passion, as the tracing the varieties and
progress of a perturbed soul.

It is to this sympathetic curiosity of our nature, exercised upon mankind in
great and trying occasions, and under the influence of the stronger passions,
when the grand, the generous, the terrible attract our attention far more than
the base and depraved, that the high and powerfully tragic, of every composition, is addressed.

This propensity is universal. Children begin to show it very early; it enters
into many of their amusements, and that part of them too, for which they show
the keenest relish. It tempts them many times, as well as the mature in years,
to be guilty of tricks, vexations, and cruelty; yet God Almighty has implanted
it within us, as well as all our other propensities and passions, for wise and good
purposes. It is our best and most powerful instructor. From it we are taught the
proprieties and decencies of ordinary life, and are prepared for distressing and
difficult situations. In examining others we know ourselves. With limbs
untorn, with head unsmitten, with senses unimpaired by despair, we know
what we ourselves might have been on the rack, on the scaffold, and in the most

afflicting circumstances of distress. Unless when accompanied with passions of the dark and malevolent kind, we cannot well exercise this disposition without becoming more just, more merciful, more compassionate; and as the dark and malevolent passions are not the predominant inmates of the human breast, it has produced more deeds – O many more! of kindness than of cruelty. It holds up for our example a standard of excellence, which, without its assistance, our inward consciousness of what is right and becoming might never have dictated. It teaches us, also, to respect ourselves, and our kind; for it is a poor mind, indeed, that from this employment of its faculties, learns not to dwell upon the noble view of human nature rather than the mean.

Universal, however, as this disposition undoubtedly is, with the generality of mankind it occupies itself in a passing and superficial way. Though a native trait of character or of passion is obvious to them as well as to the sage, yet to their minds it is but the visitor of a moment; they look upon it singly and unconnected: and though this disposition, even so exercised, brings instruction as well as amusement, it is chiefly by storing up in their minds those ideas to which the instructions of others refer, that it can be eminently useful. Those who reflect and reason upon what human nature holds out to their observation, are comparatively but few. No stroke of nature which engages their attention stands insulated and alone. Each presents itself to them with many varied connections; and they comprehend not merely the immediate feeling which gave rise to it, but the relation of that feeling to others which are concealed. We wonder at the changes and caprices of men; they see in them nothing but what is natural and accountable. We stare upon some dark catastrophe of passion, as the Indians did upon an eclipse of the moon; they, conceiving the track of ideas through which the impassioned mind has passed, regard it like the philosopher who foretold the phenomenon. Knowing what situation of life he is about to be thrown into, they perceive in the man, who, like Hazael says, 'is thy servant a dog that he should do this thing?'[3] the foul and ferocious murderer. A man of this contemplative character partakes, in some degree, of the entertainment of the gods, who were supposed to look down upon this world and the inhabitants of it, as we do upon a theatrical exhibition; and if he is of a benevolent disposition, a good man struggling with, and triumphing over adversity, will be to him, also, the most delightful spectacle. But though this eagerness to observe their fellow creatures in every situation, leads not the generality of mankind to reason and reflect; and those strokes of nature which they are so ready to remark, stand single and unconnected in their minds, yet they may be easily induced to do both: and there is no mode of instruction which they will so eagerly pursue, as that which lays open before them, in a more enlarged and connected view, than their individual observations are capable of supplying the varieties of the human mind. Above all, to be well exercised in this study will fit a man more particularly for the most important situations of life. He will prove for it the better judge, the better magistrate, the better advocate; and as a ruler or conductor of other men, under every occurring circumstance, he will find himself the better enabled to fulfil his duty, and accomplish his designs

He will perceive the natural effect of every order than he issues upon the minds of his soldiers, his subjects, or his followers; and he will deal to others judgement tempered with mercy; that is to say truly just; for justice appears to us severe only when it is imperfect.

In proportion as moral writers of every class have exercised within themselves this sympathetic propensity of our nature, and have attended to it in others, their works have been interesting and instructive. They have struck the imagination more forcibly, convinced the understanding more clearly, and more lastingly impressed the memory. If unseasoned with any reference to this, the fairy bowers of the poet, with all his gay images of delight, will be admired and forgotten; the important relations of the historian, and even the reasonings of the philosopher will make a less permanent impression.

The historian points back to the men of other ages, and from the gradually clearing mist in which they are first discovered, like the mountains of a far distant land, the generations of the world are displayed to our mind's eye in grand and regular procession. But the transactions of men become interesting to us only as we are made acquainted with men themselves. Great and bloody battles are to us battles fought in the moon, if it is not impressed upon our minds, by some circumstances attending them, that men subject to like weaknesses and passions with ourselves, were the combatants.[4]

The establishment of policy makes little impression upon us, if we are left ignorant of the beings whom they affected. Even a very masterly drawn character will but slightly imprint upon our memory the great man it belongs to, if, in the account we receive of his life, those lesser circumstances are entirely neglected, which do best of all point out to us the dispositions and tempers of men. Some slight circumstance characteristic of the particular turn of a man's mind, which at first sight seems but little connected with the great events of his life, will often explain some of those events more clearly to our understanding, than the minute details of ostensible policy. A judicious selection of those circumstances which characterize the spirit of an associated mob, paltry and ludicrous as some of them may appear, will oftentimes convey to our minds a clearer idea why certain laws and privileges were demanded and agreed to, than a methodical explanation of their causes. A historian who has examined human nature himself; and likewise attends to the pleasure which developing and tracing it, does ever convey to others, will employ our understanding as well as our memory with his pages; and if this is not done, he will impose upon the latter a very difficult task, in retaining what she is concerned with alone.

In argumentative and philosophical writings, the effect which the author's reasoning produces on our minds depends not entirely on the justness of it. The images and examples that he calls to his aid, to explain and illustrate his meaning, will very much affect the attention we are able to bestow upon it, and consequently the quickness with which we shall apprehend, and the force with which it will impress us. These are selected from animated and unanimated nature, from the habits, manners, and characters of men; and though that image or example, whatever it may be in itself, which brings out his meaning most clearly, ought to be preferred before every other, yet of two equal in this respect, that which is drawn from the most interesting source will please us the most at the time, and most lastingly take hold of our minds. An argument supported with vivid and interesting illustration will long be remembered when many equally important and clear are forgotten; and a work where many such occur will be held in higher estimation by the generality of men, than one its superior, perhaps, in acuteness, perspicuity, and good sense.

Our desire to know what men are in the closet as well as the field, by the blazing hearth, and at the social board, as well as in the council and the throne, is very imperfectly gratified by real history; romance writers, therefore, stepped boldly forth to supply the deficiency; and tale writers, and novel writers, of many descriptions, followed after. If they have not been very skilful in their delineations of nature; if they have represented men and women speaking and acting as men and women never did speak or act; if they have caricatured both our virtues and our vices; if they have given us such pure and unmixed, or such heterogeneous combinations of character as real life never presented, and yet have pleased and interested us, let it not be imputed to the dullness of man in discerning what is genuinely natural in himself. There are many inclinations belonging to us, besides this great master-propensity of which I am treating. Our love of the grand, the beautiful, the novel, and above all of the marvellous, is very strong; and if we are richly fed with what we have a good relish for, we may be weaned to forget our native and favourite aliment. Yet we can never so far forget it, but that we will cling to, and acknowledge it again, whenever it is presented before us. In a work abounding with the marvellous and unnatural, if the author has anyhow stumbled upon an unsophisticated genuine stroke of nature, we will immediately perceive and be delighted with it, though we are foolish enough to admire at the same time, all the nonsense with which it is surrounded. After all the wonderful incidents, dark mysteries, and secrets revealed, which eventful novel so liberally presents to us; after the beautiful fairy ground, and even the grand and sublime scenes of nature with which descriptive novel so often enchants us; those works which most strongly characterize human nature in the middling and lower classes of society, where it is to be discovered by stronger and more unequivocal marks, will ever be the most popular.[5] For though great pains have been taken in our higher sentimental novels to interest us in the delicacies, embarrassments, and artificial distresses of the more refined part of society, they have never been able to cope in the public opinion with these. The one is a dressed and beautiful pleasure-ground, in which we are enchanted for a while, amongst the delicate and unknown plants of artful cultivation; the other is a rough forest of our native land; the oak, the elm, the hazel, and the bramble are there; and amidst the endless varieties of its paths we can wander forever. Into whatever scenes the novelist may conduct us, what objects soever he may present to our view, still is our attention most sensibly awake to every touch faithful to nature; still are we upon the watch for everything that speaks to us of ourselves.

The fair field of what may properly be called poetry, is enriched with so many beauties, that in it we are often tempted to forget what we really are, and what kind of beings we belong to. Who in the enchanted region of simile, metaphor, allegory and description, can remember the plain order of things in this everyday world? From heroes whose majestic forms rise like a lofty tower, whose eyes are lightning, whose arms are irresistible, whose course is like the storms of heaven, bold and exalted sentiments we will readily receive; and will not examine them very accurately by that rule of nature which our own breast prescribes for us. A shepherd whose sheep, with fleeces of purest snow, browse the flowery herbage of the most beautiful valleys; whose flute is ever melodious, and whose shepherdess is ever crowned with roses; whose every care is love, will not be called very strictly to account for the loftiness and refinement of his thoughts. The fair nymph, who sighs out her sorrows to the conscious and compassionate wilds; whose eyes gleam like the bright drops of heaven; whose loose tresses stream to the breeze, may say what she pleases with impunity. I will venture, however, to say, that amidst all this decoration and ornament, all this loftiness and refinement, let one simple trait of the human heart, one expression of passion genuine and true to nature, be introduced, and it will stand forth alone in the boldness of reality, whilst the false and unnatural around it, fades away upon every side, like the rising exhalations of the morning. With admiration, and often with enthusiasm we proceed on our way through the grand and beautiful images, raised to our imagination by the lofty epic muse; but what even here are those things that strike upon the heart that we feel and remember? Neither the descriptions of war, the sound of the trumpet, the clanging of arms, the combat of heroes, nor the death of the mighty, will interest our minds like the fall of the feeble stranger, who simply expresses the anguish of his soul, at the thoughts of that far-distant home which he must never return to again, and closes his eyes amongst the ignoble and forgotten; like the timid stripling goaded by the shame of reproach, who urges his trembling steps to the fight, and falls like a tender flower before the first blast of winter. How often will some simple picture of this kind be all that remains upon our minds of the terrific and magnificent battle, whose description we have read with admiration! How comes it that we relish so much the episodes of an heroic poem? It cannot merely be that we are pleased with a resting-place, where we enjoy the variety of contrast; for were the poem of the simple and familiar kind, and an episode of the heroic style introduced into it, ninety readers out of a hundred would pass over it altogether. It is not that we meet such a story, so situated, with a kind of sympathetic good will, as in passing through a country of castles and of palaces, we should pop unawares upon some humble cottage, resembling the dwellings of our own native land, and gaze upon it with affection. The highest pleasures we receive from poetry, as well as from the real objects which surround us in the world, are derived from the sympathetic interest we all take in beings like ourselves; and I will even venture to say that were the grandest scenes which can enter into the imagination of man presented to our view and all reference to man completely shut out from our thoughts, the objects that composed it would convey to our minds little better than dry ideas of magnitude, colour, and form; and the remembrance of them would rest upon our minds like the measurement and distances of the planets.

If the study of human nature then, is so useful to the poet, the novelist, the historian, and the philosopher, of how much greater importance must it be to the dramatic writer? To them it is a powerful auxiliary, to him it is the centre and strength of the battle. If characteristic views of human nature enliven not their pages, there are many excellencies with which they can, in some degree, make up for the deficiency; it is what we receive from them with pleasure rather than demand. But in his works no richness of invention, harmony of language, nor grandeur of sentiment will supply the place of faithfully delineated nature. The poet may represent to you their great characters from the cradle to the tomb. They may represent them in any mood or temper, and under the influence of any passion which they see proper, without being obliged to put words into their mouths, those great betrayers of the feigned and adopted. They may relate every circumstance however trifling and minute, that serves to develop their tempers and dispositions. They tell us what kind of people they intend their men and women to be, and as such we receive them. If they are to move us with any scene of distress, every circumstance regarding the parties concerned in it, how they looked, how they moved, how they sighed, how the tears gushed from their eyes, how the very light and shadow fell upon them, is carefully described, and the few things that are given them to say along with all this assistance, must be very unnatural indeed if we refuse to sympathize with them. But the characters of the drama must speak directly for themselves. Under the influence of every passion, humour, and impression; in the artificial veilings of hypocrisy and ceremony, in the openness of freedom and confidence, and in the lonely hour of meditation they speak. He who made us has placed within our breast a judge that judges instantaneously of everything they say. We expect to find them creatures like ourselves; and if they are untrue to nature, we feel that we are imposed upon; as though the poet had introduced to us brethren, creatures of a different race, beings of another world.

As in other works deficiency in characteristic truth may be compensated by excellencies of a different kind, in the drama characteristic truth will compensate every other defect. Nay, it will do what appears a contradiction; one strong genuine stroke of nature will cover a multitude of sins even against nature herself. When we meet in some scene of a good play a very fine stroke of this kind, we are apt to become so intoxicated with it, and so perfectly convinced of the author's great knowledge of the human heart, that we are unwilling to suppose that the whole of it has not been suggested by the same penetrating spirit. Many well-meaning and enthusiastic critics have given themselves a great deal of trouble in this way; and have shut their eyes most ingeniously against the fair light of nature for the very love of it. They have converted, in their great zeal, sentiments palpably false, both in regard to the character and situation of the persons who utter them, sentiments which a child or a clown would detect, into the most skilful depictions of the heart. I can think of no stronger instance to show how powerfully this love of nature dwells within us. . . .

Notes

1   In confirmation of this opinion I may venture to say, that of the great numbers who go to see a public execution there are but very few who would not run away from, and avoid it, if they happened to meet with it unexpectedly. We find people stopping to look at a procession, or any other uncommon sight, they may have fallen in with accidentally, but almost never an execution. No one goes there who has not made up his mind for the occasion, which would not be the case, if any natural love of cruelty were the cause of such assemblies. [Author's note]

2   *Le Diable Boiteux* (1707), by Alain René Le Sage (1668-1747), is a picaresque novel in which a demon lifts the roof off houses. This device allows the narrator to comment satirically on the inhabitants within.

3   2 Kings 7: 11-13. Elisha shows foreknowledge of Hazael's murderous intent towards 'the children of Israel', but Hazael dissembles with his question, 'But what, is thy servant a dog, that he should do this great thing?'

4   Let two great battles be described to us with all the force and clearness of the most able pen. In the first let the most admirable exertions of military skill in the general, and the most unshaken courage in the soldiers, gain over an equal or superior number of brave opponents a complete and glorious victory. In the second let the general be less scientific, and the soldiers less dauntless. Let them go into the field for a cause that is dear to them, and fight with the ardour which such motives inspire; till discouraged with the many deaths around them, and the renovated pressure of the foe, some unlooked-for circumstance, trifling in itself, strikes their imagination at once; they are visited with the terrors of nature; their national pride, the honour of soldiership is forgotten; they fly like a fearful flock. Let some beloved chief then step forth, and call upon them by the love of their country, by the memory of their valiant fathers, by everything that kindles in the bosom of man the high and generous passions: they stop; they gather round him; and goaded by shame and indignation, returning again to the charge, with the fury of wild beasts rather than the courage of soldiers, bear down everything before them. Which of these two battles will interest us the most? and which of them shall we remember the longest? The one will stand forth in the imagination of the reader like a rock of the desert, which points out to the far-removed traveller the country through which he has passed, when its lesser objects are obscured in the distance; whilst the other leaves no traces behind it, but in the minds of the scientific in war. [Author's note]

5   Cf. William Wordsworth's analysis of the subjects that he chose for most of his poems in his and S. T. Coleridge's *Lyrical Ballads* (1798): 'Humble and rustic life was generally chosen, because, in that condition, the essential passions of the heart find a better soil in which they can attain their maturity, are less under restraint, and speak a plainer and more emphatic language . . .' (Preface to *Lyrical Ballads* (1800) in William Wordsworth, *Poetical Works*, ed. Thomas Hutchinson, new edn, rev. Ernest de Selincourt, Oxford, Oxford University Press, 1936, p. 735).

Appendix 2

'Preface' to Fugitive Verses, (1840)

In this 'Preface', Baillie allies herself with the Scottish poet, Robert Burns, as well
as asserting her distinctiveness as a poet of 'a simpler and more homely character'
than many of her contemporaries of 'these last thirty years'. She also explains that,
after a residence of fifty-seven years in London, she has removed some 'Scottish
expressions' for the sake of her English readers.

I believe myself warranted in calling the contents for the following pages
'Fugitive Verses' for by far the greatest portion has been in some way or other
already before the public, though so scattered among various publications and
collections, that it would be very difficult now for anyone but myself to bring
them together. Many of the songs are to be found in Mr George Thomson's
Collection of Irish, Welsh, and Scottish Melodies, and other Musical Works,
Both Selected and Original;[1] the Ballads, too, and many of the other occasional
pieces, are dispersed in the same way. But it would be great vanity in me to
suppose that any individual would take the trouble of drawing them from their
different lurking-places for his own private reading. This book then, does not
hold out the allurement of novelty. As among an assembly of strangers, however, we sometimes look with more goodwill upon a few recognized faces that
had been nearly lost or forgotten, though never much valued at any time, than
upon those whom we have never before beheld; so I venture to hope, that upon
the simple plea of old acquaintances, they may be received with some degree of
favour. Be this as it may, I am unwilling to quit the world and leave them
behind me in their unconnected state, or to leave the trouble of collecting and
correcting them to another – the songs written in the Scottish dialect making it
somewhat more difficult.

   The occasional pieces for the first time offered to the public, have another
disadvantage to contend with. Modern poetry, within these last thirty years,
has become so imaginative, impassioned, and sentimental, that more homely
subjects, in simple diction, are held in comparatively small estimation. This,
however, is a natural progress of the art, and the obstacles it may cast in the
way of a less gifted, or less aspiring genius, must be submitted to with good
grace. Nay, they may even sometimes be read with more relish from their very
want of the more elevated flights of fancy, from our natural love of relaxation
after having had our minds kept on the stretch, by following, or endeavouring
to follow more sublime and obscure conceptions. He who has been scouring
through the air in a balloon, or ploughing the boundless ocean in the bark of

some dauntless discoverer, or careering over the field on a warhorse, may be very well pleased after all to seat himself on a bench by his neighbour's door, and look at the meadows around him, or country people passing along the common from their daily work.[2] Let me then be encouraged to suppose that something of this nature may, with the courteous reader, operate in my behalf.

The early poems that stand first in the arrangement of this book, I now mention last. They are taken from a small volume, published by me anonymously many years ago, but not noticed by the public, or circulated in any considerable degree.[3] Indeed, in the course of after years it became almost forgotten by myself, and the feelings of my mind in a good measure coincided with the neglect it had met with. A review of those days[4] had spoken of it encouragingly, and the chief commendation bestowed was that it contained true unsophisticated representations of nature. This cheered me at the time, and then gradually faded from my thoughts. But not very long since, when I learnt from different quarters that some of the pieces from this little neglected book had found their way into collections of extracts made by those whose approbation implied some portion of real merit,[5] my little volume returned again to my own thoughts, and disposed me – on a warmly expressed opinion in its favour by a poet,[6] who, from his own refined genius, classical elegance, and high estimation with the public, is well qualified to judge – no longer to resist a latent inclination to add some of its verses to the present publication. I was the more encouraged to yield to the influence of this friend, from having formerly received unwittingly from his critical pen, very great and useful service – service that, at the beginning of my dramatical attempts, enabled me to make better head against criticism of a different character. This being decided, the difficulty was as to what pieces I ought to select; for I had a much clearer idea of those to be rejected than of those that deserved to be chosen. I hope the reader will not think with much chagrin or impatience, that admittance has been too easily granted. Those which regard the moods and passions of the human mind, and show any kindred to the works that with more success followed after, have, with a few exceptions, for this reason been preserved. When these poems were written, the author was young in years, and still younger in literary knowledge. Of all our eminent poets of modern times, not one was then known. Mr. Hayley[7] and Miss Seward,[8] and a few other cultivated poetical writers, were the poets spoken of in literary circles. Burns,[9] read and appreciated as he deserved by his own countrymen, was known to few readers south of the Tweed, where I then resided. A poet (if I dare so style myself) of a simpler and more homely character, was either, among such contemporaries, placed in a favourable or unfavourable position, as the taste and fashion of the day might direct; and I have, perhaps, no great reason to regret that my vanity was not stirred up at that time to more active exertions. Permit me to add, that in preparing them for this collection, they have undergone very little more than verbal corrections, with the expunging or alteration of a line here and there, and have never (but on one occasion noticed in a short note,) received the addition of new thoughts. Some Scottish expressions, as might naturally be expected, interfered with clearness of meaning and harmony of sound to an English reader, and some of those I have changed; but I have not been willing, unless when it appeared necessary, entirely to remove this national mark; and I believe those whom I am most ambitious to please, will not like my early verses the worse for this defect, though the difference of pronunciation in the two countries not unfrequently injures the rhyme.

Having said all that I dare to procure a lenient reception to the following pages, which contain nearly all the occasional lines, written under various circumstances and impressions of a long life, I have nothing more to urge, as I will not, from feelings that may easily be imagined, make any remarks on the latter part of the volume, appropriated to devotional and sacred subjects. To avoid any imputation of forwardness or presumption, however, I think it right to mention that those hymns marked 'For the Kirk', were written at the request of an eminent member of the Scottish Church,[10] at a time when it was in contemplation to compile by authority a new collection of hymns and sacred poetry for the general use of parochial congregations. It would have gratified me extremely to have been of the smallest service to the venerable church of my native land, which the conscientious zeal of the great majority of an intelligent and virtuous nation had founded; which their unconquerable courage, endurance of persecution, and unwearied perseverance, had reared into a church as effective for private virtue and ecclesiastical government, as any Protestant establishment in Europe. I was proud to be so occupied; my heart and my duty went along with it; but the General Assembly when afterwards applied to, refused their sanction to any new compilation, and what I had written, and many sacred verses from far better poets, proved abortive. That clergymen, who had been accustomed from their youth to hear the noble Psalms of David sung by the mingled voices of a large congregation swelling often to a sublime volume of sound, elevating the mind and quickening the feelings beyond all studied excitements of art, should regard any additions or changes as presumptuous, is a circumstance at which we ought not to be surprised.

I will no longer trouble the reader with preliminary matters. I hope the book itself will be read with a disposition to be pleased, and that even in the absence of superior merit, the variety of its subjects alone will afford some amusement.

Notes

1   George Thomson, ed., *Collection of the Songs of Burns, Sir Walter Scott, Bart, and other Eminent Lyric Poets, Ancient and Modern United to the Select Melodies of Scotland, and of Ireland and Wales, with Symphonies and Accompaniments . . . by Pleyl, Haydn, Beethoven and Kozeluck*, 6 vols, London and Edinburgh, 1822.

2   Baillie is referring here to the subjects of her own poetry.

3   *Poems: Wherein It Is Attempted to Describe Certain Views of Nature and Rustic Manners*, London, Joseph Johnson, 1790.

4   *The Monthly Review*, 6 (1791), pp. 266-9.

5   One of these anthologists was her friend and neighbour in Hampstead, the poet Anna Barbauld (1743-1825), who reprinted 'A Mother to Her Waking Infant' in *Choice Poetical Extracts* (1820).

6   Samuel Rogers (1763-1855), banker and poet, who wrote, among other works, *Poems* (1812).

7   William Hayley (1745-1820), a poet and friend of William Blake, was offered the poet laureateship in 1790, but refused this honour. His poetry is not well regarded now.

8   Anna Seward (1742-1809). See Margaret Ashmun, *The Singing Swan: An Account of Anna Seward*, New Haven, Yale University Press, and Oxford, Oxford University Press, 1931.

9   Robert Burns (1759-1796).

10   Baillie was commissioned in 1824 by the Reverend Principal Baird of the University of Edinburgh to write metrical versions of psalms for the Presbyterian Assembly, but, in the event, these hymns and psalms were never published by Baird.

Select bibliography

Readers will find my annotated bibliography of women's Romantic poetry useful in placing Joanna Baillie's poetry in the context of the Romantic period. See Jennifer Breen, 'Women Poets of the Romantic Period', in *Literature of the Romantic Period: A Bibliographical Guide*, ed. Michael O'Neill (Oxford, Oxford University Press, 1998), pp. 181-91.

Works by Joanna Baillie

Poems: Wherein it is Attempted to Describe Certain Views of Nature and Rustic Manners (London, Joseph Johnson, 1790). [Facsimile repr., in *Revolution and Romanticism Series, 1789-1834*, Oxford and New York, Woodstock Books, 1994.]

——, *A Series of Plays: In Which it is Attempted to Delineate the Stronger Passions of the Mind. Each passion being the Subject of a Tragedy and a Comedy* (London, T. Cadell, Jr, and W. Davies, 1798). [Facsimile repr., in *Revolution and Romanticism Series, 1789-1834*, Oxford and New York, Woodstock Books, 1990].

——, *A Series of Plays: In Which it is Attempted to Delineate the Stronger Passions of the Mind. Each passion being the Subject of a Tragedy and a Comedy*, Vol. 2, (London, T. Cadell, Jr, and W. Davies, 1802).

——, *Miscellaneous Plays* (London, Longman, Hurst, Rees and Orme; Edinburgh, A. Constable and Co., 1804).

——, *De Monfort; a Tragedy, in Five Acts . . . as Performed at the Theatre Royal, Drury Lane* (London, Longman, Hurst, Rees, and Orme, 1807).

——, *The Family Legend: A Tragedy* (Edinburgh, John Ballantyne and Co.; London, Longman, Hurst, Rees, and Orme, 1810).

——, *A Series of Plays: In Which it is Attempted to Delineate the Stronger Passions of the Mind, Each passion being the Subject of a Tragedy and a Comedy*, Vol. 3, (London, Longman, Hurst, Rees, Orme and Brown, 1812).

——, *Orra: A Tragedy, in Five Acts* (New York: the Longworths, 1812).

——, *Metrical Legends of Exalted Characters* (London, Longman, Hurst, Rees, Orme, and Brown, 1821).

——, *A Series of Plays: In Which it is Attempted to Delineate the Stronger Passions of the Mind, Each Passion being the Subject of a Tragedy and a Comedy*, new edn, 3 vols (London, Longman, Hurst, Rees, Orme, and Brown, 1821).

——, ed., *A Collection of Poems* (London, Longman, Hurst, Rees, Orme and Brown, 1823).

——, *The Martyr: A Drama, in Three Acts* (London, Longman, Rees, Orme, Brown, and Green, 1826).

——, *The Bride; a Drama, in Three Acts* (London, Henry Colburn, 1828).

——, *The Complete Poetical Works* (Philadelphia, Carey and Lea, 1832).

——, *Fugitive Verses* (London, Edward Moxon, 1840).

——, *The Dramatic and Poetical Works* (London, Longman, Brown and Green and Longmans, 1851).

MSS collections

Baillie, Joanna, *Poems* (17– or 18–), Hunter-Baillie Collection, Vol. 1, nos 44-8 and 75, London, Royal College of Surgeons Library.

——, *Prose Writings* (17– or 18–), Hunter-Baillie Collection, Vol. 9, nos 10 and 68-9, London, Royal College of Surgeons Library.

——, *40 Letters* (1802 or 1833 and undated), Hunter-Baillie Collection, Vol. 9, London, Royal College of Surgeons Library.

——, letter to Henrietta Baillie, Hunter-Baillie Collection, Vol. 2, no. 46, London, Royal College of Surgeons Library.

——, letters to Lady Bentham (1805-1837), BL Add. MSS 33544-33546.

——, two letters to Mary Berry (1812 and undated), Hunter-Baillie Collection, Vol. 2, nos 39 and 70, London, Royal College of Surgeons Library.

——, *Recollections: Written at the Request of Miss Berry*, 1831, Hunter-Baillie Collection, Vol. 2, no. 56, London, Royal College of Surgeons Library.

——, letter to George Crabbe (1822), Brotherton Library, Leeds, Brotherton Collection; extra-illustrated Crabbe volumes, 4, pp. 120-2.

——, letter to Elizabeth Frere, 1838, BL Add. MS 46138, f. 213.

——, letters to Margaret Holford, Camden Borough Library, London.

——, letters to George Thomson (1804-1842), BL Add. MSS 33544-33546.

——, letter to Miss Tytler, 1836, BL Add. MS. 42575, f. 28.

——, letter to Rev. B. White (17– or 18–), John Rylands University Library of Manchester, English MS, 372/89.

Anthologies and editions of poetry

Ashfield, Andrew, ed., *Romantic Women Poets, 1770-1838*, Vol. 1 (Manchester, Manchester University Press, 1994; rev. edn 1998).

——, *Romantic Women Poets, 1788-1848*, Vol. 2 (Manchester, Manchester, Manchester University Press, 1998).

Breen, Jennifer, ed., *Women Romantic Poets, 1785-1832: An Anthology* (London, Everyman / Dent, 1992; new edn 1994).

——, *Women Romantics 1785-1832: Writing in Prose* (London, Everyman / Dent, 1996).

Burns, Robert, *The Poems and Songs of Robert Burns*, 3 vols, ed. James Kinsley (London, Oxford University Press, 1970).

Crabbe, George, *Selected Poems*, ed. Gavin Edwards (Harmondsworth, Penguin, 1991).

Lonsdale, Roger, ed., *The New Oxford Book of Eighteenth-Century Verse* (Oxford, Oxford University Press, 1984).

——, *Eighteenth-Century Women Poets: An Oxford Anthology* (Oxford, Oxford University Press, 1989).

McGann, Jerome, ed., *The New Oxford Book of Romantic Period Verse* (Oxford, Oxford University Press, 1993).

Milford Humphrey, ed., *The Oxford Book of Romantic Verse* (London, Oxford University Press, 1901).

Thomson, George, *Collection of the Songs of Burns, Sir Walter Scott, Bart, and other Eminent Lyric Poets Ancient and Modern United to the Select Melodies of Scotland, and of Ireland and Wales, with Symphonies and Accompaniments . . . by Pleyel, Haydn, Beethoven and Kozeluck*, 6 vols (London and Edinburgh, 1822).

Turner, Katherine, ed., *Selected Poems of Thomas Grey, Charles Churchill and William Cowper* (Harmondsworth, Penguin, 1997).

Wordsworth, William, *Poetical Works*, ed. Thomas Hutchinson, new edn, rev. Ernest de Selincourt (London, Oxford University Press, 1936).

Wu, Duncan (ed.), *Romantic Women Poets: An Anthology* (Oxford, Blackwell, 1997).

Bibliographies, checklists and dictionaries

The Location Register of Eighteenth- and Nineteenth-Century English Literary MSS and Letters (London, British Library, 1995).

Alston, R. C., comp., *A Checklist of Women Writers, 1801-1900: Fiction, Verse, Drama* (London, British Library, 1990).

Blain, Virginia, Clements, Patricia, and Grundy, Isobel (eds), *The Feminist Companion to Literature in English: Women Writers from the Middle Ages to the Present* (London, Batsford, 1990).

Jackson, J. R. De J. Jackson, comp., *Romantic Poetry by Women: A Bibliography, 1770-1835* (Oxford, Oxford University Press, 1993).

Robinson, Mairi, ed., *The Concise Scots Dictionary* (Edinburgh, Chambers Harrap, 1985).

Sykes, J. B., ed., *The Concise Oxford Dictionary*, 6th edn (Oxford, Oxford University Press, 1976).

Thorne, J. O. and Collocott, T. L. eds, *Chambers Biographical Dictionary* (Edinburgh, Chambers, rev. 1984).

Todd, Janet, ed., *A Dictionary of Women Writers* (London, Routledge, 1989).

Dictionary of National Biography.

Biography, essays and commentary

Armstrong, Isobel, 'The Gush of the Feminine: How Can We Read Women's Poetry of the Romantic Period?', in *Romantic Women Writers: Voices and Counter-voices*, ed. Paula R. Feldman and Theresa M. Kelley (Hanover and London, University Press of New England, 1995), pp. 13-32.

Bold, Valentina, 'Beyond "The Empire of the Gentle Heart": Scottish Women Poets of the Nineteenth-Century', in *A History of Scottish Women's Writing*, ed. Douglas Gifford and Dorothy McMillan (Edinburgh, Edinburgh University Press, 1997), pp. 246-61.

Breen, Jennifer, 'Women Romantic Poets', in *Times Higher Education Supplement*, 4 May 1990.

Brown, Marshall, 'Romanticism and Enlightenment', in *The Cambridge Companion to British Romanticism*, ed. Stuart Curran (Cambridge, Cambridge University Press, 1993), pp. 25-47.

Burroughs, Catherine B., 'English Romantic Women Writers and Theatre Theory: Joanna Baillie's Prefaces to the *Plays on the Passions*' in *Revisioning Romanticism: British Women Writers, 1776-1837*, ed. Carol Shiner Wilson and Joel Haefner (Philadelphia, University of Pennsylvania Press, 1994), pp. 274-96.

——, '"Out of the Pale of Social Kindred Cast": Conflicted Performance Style in Joanna Baillie's *De Monfort*', in *Romantic Women Writers: Voices and Counter-voices*, ed. Paula R. Feldman and Theresa M. Kelley (Hanover and London, University Press of New England, 1995), pp. 223-35.

Butler, Marilyn, *Romantics, Rebels and Reactionaries: English Literature and its Background, 1760-1830* (Oxford, Oxford University Press, 1981).

Carhart, Margaret S., *The Life and Work of Joanna Baillie* (New Haven, Yale University Press, and London, Oxford University Press, 1923).

Curran, Stuart, 'Romantic Poetry: The "I" Altered', in *Romanticism and Feminism*, ed. Anne Mellor (Bloomington, Indiana University Press, 1988), p. 186.

Davie, Donald, *The Eighteenth-Century Hymn in England* (Cambridge, Cambridge University Press, 1993).

Dawson, P. M. S., 'Poetry in an Age of Revolution', in *The Cambridge Companion to British Romanticism*, ed. Stuart Curran (Cambridge, Cambridge University Press, 1993), pp. 48-73.

Ferguson, Moira, *Subject to Others: British Woman Writers and Colonial Slavery, 1670-1834* (New York and London, Routledge, 1992).

Gilroy, Amanda, 'From Here to Alterity: The Geography of Femininity in the Poetry of Joanna Baillie', in *A History of Scottish Women's Writing*, ed. Douglas Gifford and Dorothy McMillan (Edinburgh, Edinburgh University Press, 1997), pp. 143-57.

Jones, M. G., *Hannah More* (Cambridge, Cambridge University Press, 1952).

Lambertson, Chester Lee, *The Letters of Joanna Baillie (1801-1832)*, unpublished Ph D dissertation, Harvard University, Cambridge, Massachusetts, 1956.

Lindsay, Maurice, *History of Scottish Literature*, (London, Hale, 1977, rev. 1992).

Mellor, Anne K. *Romanticism and Gender* (New York and London, Routledge, 1993).

McCue, Kirsten, 'Women and Song 1750-1850', in *A History of Scottish Women's Writing*, ed. Douglas Gifford and Dorothy McMillan (Edinburgh, Edinburgh University Press, 1997), pp. 58-70.

McGann, Jerome, *The Politics of Sensibility: A Revolution in Literary Style* (Oxford, Oxford University Press, 1996; paperback 1998).

McKerrow, Mary, 'Joanna Baillie and Mary Brunton: Women of the Manse', in *Living by the Pen: Early British Women Writers*, ed. Dale Spender (New York and London, Teachers College Press, 1992), pp. 160-74.

Patten, Janice, 'Joanna Baillie, *A Series of Plays*', in *A Companion to Romanticism*, ed. Duncan Wu (Oxford, Blackwell, 1998), pp. 169-78.

Purinton, Marjean D., *Romantic Ideology Unmasked: The Mentally Constructed Tyrannies in Dramas of William Wordsworth, Lord Byron, Percy Shelley, and Joanna Baillie* (Newark, Del., 1994).

Roberts, William, ed., *Memoirs of the Life and Correspondence of Mrs Hannah More*, 3 vols (London, R. B. Seeley and W. Burnside, 3rd edn 1835).

Ross, Marlon B., *The Contours of Masculine Desire: Romanticism and the Rise of Women's Poetry* (New York and Oxford, Oxford University Press, 1989).

Scullion, Adrienne, 'Some Women of the Nineteenth-Century Scottish Theatre: Joanna Baillie, Frances Wright and Helen MacGregor', in *A History of Scottish Women's Writing*, ed. Douglas Gifford and Dorothy McMillan (Edinburgh, Edinburgh University Press, 1997), pp. 158-78.

Speck, W. A., *Literature and Society in Eighteenth-Century England: Ideology, Politics and Culture, 1680-1820* (Harlow, Addison Wesley Longman, 1998).

Williamson, Karina, 'The Eighteenth Century and the Sister Choir', *Essays in Criticism: A Quarterly Journal of Literary Criticism* (Oxford, 1990), October, 40:4, 271-86.

Wordsworth, Jonathan, *The Bright Work Grows: Women Writers of the Romantic Age*, 'Revolution and Romanticism Series, 1789-1834' (Poole, Woodstock Books), 1997.

——, 'Ann Yearsley to Caroline Norton: Women Poets of the Romantic Period', *Wordsworth Circle* (Grasmere, 1995), 26:3, 114-24.

Wordsworth, William, 'Preface' to *Lyrical Ballads* (1800) in *Poetical Works*, ed. Thomas Hutchinson, new edn, rev. Ernest de Selincourt (London, Oxford University Press), 1936, pp. 734-41.

Index of first lines